# GARDENING FOR GEEKS

# GARDENING FOR GEEKS

# DIY TESTS, GADGETS, & TECHNIQUES

*that utilize microbiology, mathematics, and ecology to exponentially maximize the yield of your garden*

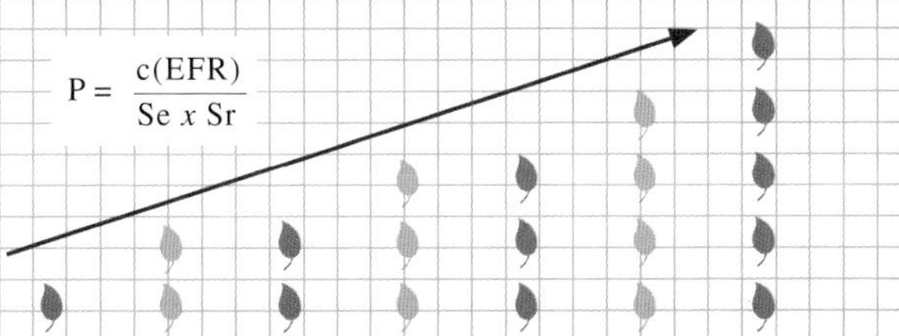


FEATURES INFORMATION ON:

- WATER CATCHMENT
- VERTICAL GARDENING
- BIO-INTENSIVE METHODS


Christy Wilhelmi

Founder of Gardenerd.com

Published by
Adams Media, a division of F+W Media, Inc.
57 Littlefield Street, Avon, MA 02322. U.S.A.
*www.adamsmedia.com*

ISBN 10: 1-4405-5779-9
ISBN 13: 978-1-4405-5779-8
eISBN 10: 1-4405-5780-2
eISBN 13: 978-1-4405-5780-4

Printed in the United States of America.

10 9 8 7 6 5 4 3 2 1

Readers are urged to take all appropriate precautions before undertaking any how-to task. Always read and follow instructions and safety warnings for all tools and materials, and call in a professional if the task stretches your abilities too far. Although every effort has been made to provide the best possible information in this book, neither the publisher nor the author are responsible for accidents, injuries, or damage incurred as a result of tasks undertaken by readers. This book is not a substitute for professional services.

Many of the designations used by manufacturers and sellers to distinguish their product are claimed as trademarks. Where those designations appear in this book and Adams Media was aware of a trademark claim, the designations have been printed with initial capital letters.

Photographs by Christy Wilhelmi unless otherwise indicated.

*This book is available at quantity discounts for bulk purchases.*
*For information, please call 1-800-289-0963.*

For Mom and Dad

## Acknowledgments

There are so many geeks to thank, and numerous shoulders I leaned on throughout the process of writing this book. First and foremost, my patient and marvelous husband Andrew Cheeseman, who put up with months of neglect and take-out food while I threw myself headlong into this project. His well-trained grammar-geek eyes and physicist/math brain helped hone these pages. To Hexie Cheeseman and Suzy Wright, for being two more sets of eyes proofing my work, thanks so much for your invaluable help. To the ladies of my "writers' group," all unwavering cheerleaders, your encouragement and knowledge of the writing world made this much easier. To Jonathan Blank, who knows a thing or two about book publishing and willingly spent time sharing it with me, I cannot thank you enough.

I must draw particular attention to the garden geeks who have inspired my gardening exploits throughout the years (in no particular order): John Jeavons, Mel Bartholomew, the late Geoff Hamilton, Rosalind Creasy, Michael Pollen, David King, Jere Gettle, Louise Riotte, Barbara Kingsolver, and everyone at Ocean View Farms organic community garden. To those who helped clarify the material for this book, I appreciate the access you afforded me: Victoria Boudman of the Square Foot Gardening Foundation, Eben Fodor of SunWorks, master preserver Rose Lawrence of Red Bread Bakery, irrigation wunderkind Russell Ackerman, and again, John Jeavons of Ecology Action.

Special thanks to Martha Brown at UC Santa Cruz and David Rosenstein of EVO Farm for taking the time to show me around their fabulously geeky gardens. Last but never least I must thank my parents, Frank and Jo Wilhelmi, for being the engineer/carpenter and nurse/wonder-cook geeks who begat this geek.

# CONTENTS

# INTRODUCTION

# What's It All About?

When garden geeks get excited about a subject, they want to know everything. Gardening is an exciting topic—a vast world of soil biology, botany, and horticulture. It cross-pollinates with the insect world, meteorology, and nutrition. The more we learn about gardening, the more we realize there is to learn. It's a wonderfully addictive passion to have.

Do you want to know *everything*? This is a great place to start, but keep in mind that gardening knowledge doesn't arrive in a specific sequence. With the exception of the seasonal calendar or a planting schedule, gardening is not linear. It shifts each year, challenging us to figure out nature's next step. It tests our instincts as much as our knowledge, and in the end nature always wins. Most of the time we benefit from nature's triumph, but just like Olympic athletes, garden geeks experience both the thrill of victory and the agony of defeat.

This book is meant to be a geeky gateway into all things cool about gardening. It gives you the basics to start designing and building the garden of your dreams. It also will lead you to bigger concepts to explore later, when you're ready. It delves into the science of how plants work, how soil lives, and how bugs help. Even though it takes you step by step through the process, I encourage you to jump around through the book. Early on, you'll notice references to later chapters. If you can't wait, feel free to jump forward and read. Whatever floats your boat!

The information in this book is compiled from several classes I teach, with extra-added nerdy details that don't fit into the confines of the classroom. Students have been asking me to put it all down in one place. Well, here it is. Have at it. I hope you enjoy this journey into the geeky side of gardening. Put on your gloves and let's get started.

Happy gardening!

Seeds
Seeds
Seeds

# CHAPTER 1

# CREATING YOUR GARDEN ECOSYSTEM

There are many things to consider when planning a garden. Location is everything, but not the only thing. Sure, it's important to make sure your garden will get enough sun (a minimum of six hours per day), but let's talk about the other factors. Let's talk about your garden ecosystem. After all, your garden is a community of living things, and for it to flourish, they'll all have to get along together.

Wherever your garden is located, be it on a balcony, patio, or backyard, you will want to create an environment that supports your efforts. Your garden's ecosystem can provide shelter, windbreaks, and even pest control assistance if you include a few key elements. From simple to more complex, the following components all play a role in that ecosystem.

## Habitats

Established trees are an important part of your garden's ecosystem. Not only do they absorb carbon dioxide and release oxygen for a healthier planet, but they also provide a place for birds and insects to live. Ants and other insects crawl through the tree's bark, and birds take advantage of that traffic. Birds build nests and lay their young, or visit on their way to higher latitudes. Then they scavenge your garden for food, and in the process they provide pest management services for you, gobbling up bugs and worms.

You can help provide a reason for birds to congregate in your garden by hanging bird feeders and seed cakes. Birdhouses, made from gourds or wood, provide a habitat as well. Many gardeners grow sunflowers, which develop dinner-plate-sized seed heads, to attract birds. While it's true that these winged creatures will enjoy your sunflowers whether you want them to or not, the benefits of having birds in the garden generally outweigh the negative effects.

### Bats

Bats, if you have them in your neck of the woods, help reduce the pest population by swooping through the sky at dusk like airborne vacuum cleaners, eating bugs in mid-flight. According to Bat Conservation International, bats consume "night-flying insects, including many of the most damaging agricultural pests . . . A single little brown bat can eat up to 1,000 mosquito-sized insects in a single hour." Bats serve other purposes as well. Did you know they are pollinators? As they drink nectar from flowers, they help pollinate many cacti and fruiting plants. As a bonus, they leave behind droppings called *guano*, which happens to be among the best fertilizers around. Bat droppings include 11–16 percent nitrogen, 8–12 percent phosphoric acid, and 2–3 percent potash—all components of healthy soil. Guano can also serve as a composting starter and a fungicide.

If you are reluctant to welcome bats into your world, this is a good time to let go of creepy bat stereotypes. With bat populations in serious decline, they need all the help they can get. You can install a bat house on a wall under the eaves of a home, garage, or shed to encourage bats to take up residence. Bat houses are narrow boxes with even narrower compartments inside (about ¾" deep) that allow bats a place of safe, dark shelter. In a study published in *The Bat House Researcher* in spring, 2004, it was revealed bats prefer larger bat houses (at least 20" wide × 25" high) that are painted and mounted on a building, rather than mounted on a post or trees. You can find several free plans for building your own bat house, along with tips for attracting bats, on the Bat Conservation International website, *www.Batcon.org.*

### Toads

Toads are another great addition, and pest consumer, for your garden. They consume slugs (yay!) and worms (like nasty cutworms that mow down your kale plants before the seedlings ever reach harvesting size). Granted, toads don't inhabit every climate zone, but where there is moisture and shelter, they often make a home. Make a toad house out of a terra-cotta pot by chipping off a wedge of the upper rim of the pot. Turn the pot over, nestle it into a grassy corner, and *voilà!* You have a toad house with a little entryway. Provide some kind of water source, like a fountain or shallow pond, and toads will find your garden very desirable.

### Bees

Bees are critically important to our garden ecosystem. They are responsible for pollinating a huge percentage of crops, constituting one out of every three bites of food we eat. Without bees, we wouldn't have many of the fruits and vegetables we bring to the table. The presence of bees in your garden can boost yields between 10 and 50 percent, according to independent studies on a variety of crops. Even crops that don't require bees in order to set fruit appear to benefit. Cheryl Miller of Sustainable Harvest International reported on coffee farmers in Honduras for the Rodale Institute. She explained that "coffee plants are capable of self-pollination, so for a long time researchers did not think insects made much difference to the crop. But studies show that when bees pollinate coffee plants, yields can increase by more than 50 percent."

Courtesy of *www.HoneyLove.org.*

Farmers hire beekeepers to bring hives to their fields, but urban beekeeping is gaining popularity with home gardeners. As Colony Collapse Disorder (CCD) continues to decimate the world's bee population (theories about what causes it range from cell phones, to mites, to pesticides), gardeners are taking the fight into their own hands by setting up beehives as part of their ecosystem. Some place a hive on the roof, while others situate their hives in a corner of the backyard, pointing toward a wall to direct bees upward on a path away from humans.

To encourage bees and other beneficial insects, grow beneficial flowers. What the heck are those, you ask? Let's take a closer look.

**GEEKY GARDENING TIP**

**BE ONE WITH THE BEE**

Bees only become aggressive if their hive is being threatened. Many gardeners enjoy tending their garden while bees hover nearby. Bees come and go as they please, pollinating your vegetables and fruit trees, increasing yields, and leaving behind a legacy of bountiful harvests.

## Beneficial Flowers and Their Friends

Some beneficial flowers attract pollinators, such as bees and wasps, to the garden. Other types of flowers attract insect predators, such as parasitic wasps (about the size of a gnat) and praying mantises. Still another type of flower works like a trap crop, excreting an odor that attracts pests to the plant instead of to your valuable crops. Calendula or nasturtiums, for example, are reliable trap crops, because they have a strong scent and it isn't uncommon to find them infested with aphids. Great! Leave those aphids right there. Now they aren't destroying your broccoli plants. With trap crops, you can isolate pests to one area of your garden and avoid using sprays to control their populations.

## No More Pests?

But why not just wipe them out altogether? Good question, and the answer is even better. If you eliminate pests completely, then the beneficial insects will have nothing to eat. Remember, your ecosystem is all about balance. Have the right balance of ingredients (in this case, pests versus beneficial insects) and your garden will achieve a balance all its own. You won't have to work as hard to keep pests under control, and you'll be able to

Nasturtiums act as a trap crop to lure pests to their flowers instead of your veggies.

enjoy more of your harvest in an unmolested state. We'll discuss specific plants to include in your ecosystem later in the Pest Control chapter under Good Bugs Versus Bad Bugs. For now, just know that planting flowers can be beneficial to your garden's health.

Where should you plant them? Just like trees, beneficial flowers function wonderfully as a hedge or border to your garden. Plant flowers around the perimeter to encourage insects to make a home there. Flowers can also be planted between crops to assist with pest control in planter beds. A combination of both scenarios will help ensure balance.

## BUILD A SWARM BOX FOR BEES

If you want to dive into urban beekeeping or invite bees into your ecosystem, start by attracting a swarm to your garden. It's not as scary as it sounds. You can mail order bees, but it's expensive. It's actually better to attract one that may be passing through, or one that frequents your yard already. When swarms are looking for a new home, they are at the least aggressive stage in life because they don't have a home or offspring to protect. A swarm box provides a temporary habitat in which bees can congregate (instead of inside your wall or water meter box). Once you've collected a swarm in the box, you (or better yet, a local beekeeper) can transfer the colony to a proper hive that will live on your property.

*Www.HoneyLove.org*, a nonprofit urban beekeeping organization in Los Angeles, California, dedicates thousands of hours per year to educating residents about keeping bees. It has spearheaded a campaign to make beekeeping legal in their county, and spend countless hours rescuing bees from "unsupported" locations. If a homeowner finds a swarm living in his walls,

HoneyLove is one of many organizations that will come and remove the colony without killing the bees. The founders of HoneyLove strive to find a home for the bees with a farmer or homeowner in an area where beekeeping is legal.

Rob McFarland of HoneyLove explains that "swarming happens when a thriving colony of bees has outgrown its home. The existing queen and 60 percent of the worker bees exit the hive in search of a new dark hollow space to colonize, leaving the remaining bees with all the essentials to build the colony back up—honey, pollen, brood (baby bees), and a virgin queen." Swarm boxes can be made from a plethora of materials, including untreated wood (no particle board, please), cardboard boxes, and even wicker baskets. Bees are looking for a hollow cavity between 8 and 10½ gallons, which equates to a box about 10" high × 20" wide × 10" deep. Be sure to include a small access hole (about 1¼" in diameter) on one side of the box, near the

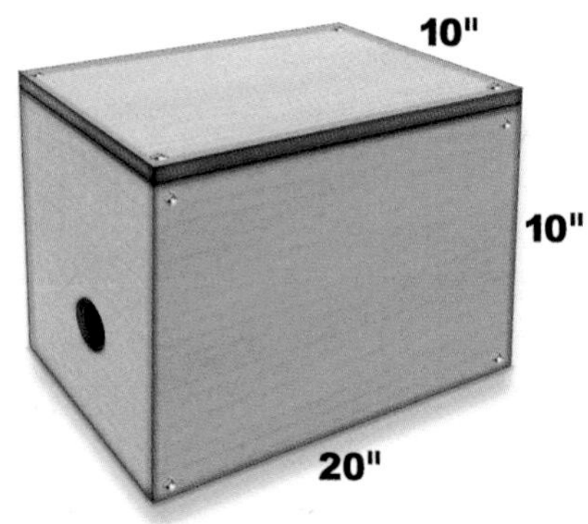


**A basic swarm box.** Images and content contribution courtesy of *www.HoneyLove.org.*

bottom. You'll also need a way to cover the hole once bees inhabit the box. The top of the box is screwed rather than nailed on, to make it easier to open the container when it's full of bees.

Some sources suggest hanging foundationless frames inside the box. These are either strips of wood that sit along the top, inside the box (usually coated with a narrow line of beeswax to encourage bees to build a comb there), or wood frames that do not contain a starter sheet of beeswax. The box shown here doesn't use frames or strips.

Indigenous communities have made swarm boxes out of wicker baskets (like a small office trash can) covered securely with a sheet of plywood on top. These baskets, as well as the more formal wooden boxes, can be attached to a tree for awaiting bees. You can nail a flat piece of wood to the back of the swarm box that extends above the box for several inches. Drill a ½" hole in the extension and hang it on a tree from a nail. You can also secure it on a thick branch. Either way, you will want to make it easy to remove the box when it is full of bees.

There are two other key ingredients in the swarm box: a cotton swab with a dab of lemongrass oil inside, and a nearby source of water. Bees get thirsty and will go elsewhere unless they have access to water. Check your swarm box for a colony weekly and when it's been colonized, get help moving the bees to a proper hive box. Then get ready for higher yields in the garden.

## Garden Orientation

Get out your compass; it's time to determine the best orientation for your garden. If you live in the northern hemisphere, a south-facing garden is best (in the southern hemisphere, of course, the opposite is true). The sun rises in the east, and because the earth's axis is tilted, the sun travels across the sky from east to west at a southerly angle. Therefore, if your garden is situated so it is exposed to that southerly arc of the sun's path, your garden will get the full-sun exposure—at least six hours per day—that is required to grow vegetables. Many times, situating a garden at the northernmost point of the yard allows for the best southerly exposure. If your yard is shadowed by trees or tall buildings, the best location for a garden may indeed be your front yard. The open streets often allow for unobstructed full-sun gardening.

In the winter, the sun's arc is lower in the sky, so shadows from surrounding buildings or trees will be longer. Take this into account when planning out your location if you live in a climate where winter gardening is feasible. If the only space available gets sun in the summer, but is in shadow in the winter, consider planting crops that do well in partial sunlight or shade during that time. Swiss chard, kale, strawberries, and many herbs will tolerate partial shade.

Another thing to consider when plotting out your planter beds or rows is their orientation. Again, full-sun exposure is the goal. If you lay out your beds or rows with the longest sides running east

### GEEKY GARDENING TIP

#### COMPASS ALTERNATIVE

If you don't have a compass, you can use your favorite Internet map search on a desktop computer and type in your address. The top of the results page, regardless of satellite or map view, always points north. Zoom in close enough to see your property, and assess which direction your garden faces.

to west (yes, this is contrary to what some experts say), your plants will have equal access to that full southern exposure as the sun crosses the sky. For example, let's say you have a 4'× 8' raised bed. Orient the bed so that the long side, the 8' length, runs from east to west. Why does this really matter? The answer lies in the next part of planning your garden's orientation.

## Plant Placement

Once your garden is laid out, you can start planning which plants go where. This may seem obvious, but it's a bit of a trick to ensure the best sun exposure for your plants. It's time to think about the vegetables you want to grow in terms of their height. For best results, place tall and trellised plants toward the north, and shorter or trailing plants to the south. Again, in the southern hemisphere, these directions should be reversed.

- **Tall and trellised crops:** asparagus, corn, cucumbers, fava or bell beans, grains (wheat, quinoa, oats, etc.), melons (see Chapter 8, Keeping Order), peas, pole beans, and tomatoes.
- **Medium crops:** most brassicas (broccoli, cauliflower, cabbages, kale, collards, etc.), celery, eggplant, garlic, leeks, okra, onions, shallots, peppers, potatoes, and Swiss chard.
- **Short and trailing crops:** arugula, most herbs, kohlrabi, lettuces, root crops (carrots, parsnips, beets, etc.), radishes, spinach, summer squash (i.e., zucchini, yellow crookneck), winter squash (i.e., pumpkins, acorn), and watermelon.

By placing shorter crops in front of (or to the south of) taller crops, all plants have access to full sun and won't compete or overtake one another. Let's take that same 4' × 8' raised bed and plan out the crops to be planted here.

**Note: Reverse this in the southern hemisphere.**

↑ N

| | | | | | |
|---|---|---|---|---|---|
| Tall Crops | Tomato | Tomato | Tomato | Cucumber | Cucumber |
| Medium Crops | Pepper | Pepper | Pepper | Eggplant | Swiss Chard |
| Short Crops | Lettuce | Lettuce | Spinach | Radishes | Arugula |

### Tallest to Shortest

Tall crops like tomatoes and cucumbers, which can be trellised, are located in the back or to the north of the raised bed. Medium crops, such as peppers, eggplant, and Swiss chard, are placed in front of the tallest crops, closer to the south. Finally, the shortest crops, like lettuces, spinach, carrots, radishes, and arugula, are placed in the southernmost part at the front of the raised bed. This allows all the vegetables to access full sun.

Now for the cool part—literally. This plant placement method can also be used to strategize in hot weather, to protect plants that can't handle extreme temperatures in the summer months. For example, lettuces bolt to seed quickly in hot weather, making them bitter and inedible. You can strategically grow cucumbers on a trellis in the middle of the raised bed, in the medium row, and then plant lettuces to the north or behind the cucumbers in the shadows of the plants. *Ta-da!* A cucumber sun umbrella. The lettuces will stay cooler during hotter weather and resist the urge to peter out so quickly.

Planting short or trailing crops to the south also has a benefit. When it comes to trailing crops like zucchini and watermelons, they can take over your entire garden without much effort. Usually, these trailing crops tend to grow toward the sun. So by planting them toward the south end of the raised bed, the vines will gravitate southward, into your pathways instead of consuming precious space in your raised bed. This will leave room for other crops without sacrificing an entire bed. Vigorous plants will still attempt to sprawl all over the place, but you can easily move the vines out of the way, since they only attach to the ground at the roots.

## Special Considerations for Wildlife and Extreme Temperatures

If you live in foothill, mountainous, or recently developed areas where deer, raccoons, or ground-dwelling animals reside, you may need to take additional steps when setting up your garden. It's possible you'll need to construct fencing, underground barriers, or even a walk-in structure in order to protect your garden. If you're going to put in all the effort to grow some of your own food, you might as well reap the benefit of being able to harvest it all. And let's not forget household pets. A low barrier may not be enough to keep Scruffy from trampling your raised beds and eating your tomatoes (yep, they do that). Most of these protections will be discussed in the Pest Control chapter, but keep this in mind as you plan out your gardening area.

If your region experiences frost or high temperatures for extended periods of time, you may want to include overhead protection for your crops. Desert communities often use shade structures to protect their plants from scorching during hot summers. Simple metal frames or PVC hoops can be covered with shade cloth to block out 30–70 percent of sunlight. When temperatures drop, shade cloth can be replaced with insulated garden fabric. We'll talk more about this in the Garden Beds chapter.

# CHAPTER 2

# GARDEN BEDS

Once you have your garden location, orientation, and general area planned, it's time to get to work on building the garden itself. This chapter will explain the reasoning behind using raised beds as well as the different options for materials. We'll also cover the specifics of how to build your garden beds and offer tricks for building beds that will last.

## Why Raised Beds?

Raised beds are a great way to organize your garden; they offer a clear delineation between growing areas and pathways, but

most of the benefits reach beyond aesthetics. In climates where the ground freezes in winter, raised beds are essential. By elevating the planting area above ground, the bed soil will thaw and drain more quickly in spring, allowing for an earlier start to your gardening endeavors.

If you have heavy clay soil (read more about that in the All about Soil chapter), raised beds can alleviate the days of backbreaking labor required to set up a garden, as well as to condition the soil each year. Raised beds don't eliminate work altogether, but they make it much easier to add compost and improve soil structure and tilth as time goes on. In some cases, once you've built your raised beds, you may never need a shovel again. A hand trowel will often suffice for working the soil and planting crops.

## Fight Droughts

If you choose to set up your garden with raised beds, you will also notice they save time and valuable resources. Raised beds concentrate the areas that need water, so rather than watering your entire garden area, you're only watering what's in the raised beds. Since water is a precious resource, and droughts are predicted to become more frequent and long lasting in places that already experience them, it makes sense to put water only where it is needed. As a result, your pathways remain dry. Dry pathways mean fewer weeds, which equals less work for you. Mulch those pathways with wood chips or other biodegradable materials (newspaper, straw, and burlap sacks work well), and you will even further reduce the need to weed.

Raised beds are the method of choice for most bio-intensive gardening methods (more about those in Chapter 5) because they concentrate resources and allow a gardener to maintain the beds without walking on and compressing the soil. Raised beds are also handy for folks with lower back issues or certain disabilities. The elevated surface area makes it easier to garden without bending over as far, and oftentimes you can build beds tall enough to prevent bending altogether. Elevated raised beds (up on legs) can be built for wheelchair accessibility. See? The benefits really do go on and on.

## Materials for Raised Beds

When it comes to deciding which materials to use for building a raised bed, you've got a lot of options, depending on your budget and needs. If you strive to recycle and reuse found materials, then "urbanite" or broken concrete might be the way to go. If you're in a tight space, thinner materials that allow for the most gardening space with the least bulk—wood or composite lumber—are a better choice. Let's take a look at the possibilities.

**Raised bed made from two levels of 2" × 6" Trex decking. With no known gophers in the neighborhood, chicken wire was used simply as a precaution. In the end it was not needed.**

### Wood

This can be assembled quickly and lasts for years, depending on the type of wood you use. Douglas fir, which is relatively inexpensive, lasts about three to five years before it begins to decompose (though some have seen it last over ten years in dry conditions). If you are building a simple frame for an experimental garden, or plan to move in a few years, Douglas fir is good enough to use.

Redwood is a more durable option for wood-framed raised beds. It is an acidic wood, which makes it naturally antimicrobial. Redwood raised beds tend to last about ten to fifteen years longer than Douglas fir beds.

Cedar, which lasts twenty years or more, is a great option for long-term raised beds. It can be more expensive but is worth the investment if you plan to be in the same place for a while. Cedar resists decay and is often available as rough-cut lumber, which means it hasn't been milled down to the standard (think thinner) dimensions. The thicker wood is more rustic, but those extra millimeters make it even more durable.

### Composite Lumber

Composite lumber is another option for planter beds. This type of material is a blend of recycled plastic packaging waste and wood pulp. It is extruded into the shape of wood and is usually used to build decks and patios. Many companies offer prefabricated raised beds made from nonleaching and soil-safe composite lumber, but be aware that not all composite lumbers are safe for direct soil contact. Trex decking, made by Trex Company *(www.trex.com)*, is one of the few composite lumbers that specifically states it is safe for direct soil contact. Some composite lumbers begin to disintegrate when they come in contact with soil. Veranda, a thinner composite product found on the shelves of larger hardware stores, clearly states it is not safe for direct soil contact.

Composite lumber like Trex has its advantages. It's long lasting (Trex is guaranteed for twenty-five years but is likely to last even longer), it won't splinter, and you never need to paint or stain it. The material costs about a third more than wood, but given the durability, it's worth the expense to know you won't have to build another raised bed for a very long time, if ever again. Composites are dense and heavy, so you may blow through a saw blade or two while cutting it, but in all other respects it cuts and behaves like wood.

### Urbanite or Concrete Blocks

These are popular options for those who are looking to use recycled products. If you spy your neighbors breaking out their driveway or sidewalk, ask if you can have the broken pieces. These concrete bits are great for building retaining walls that are thick and sturdy. They can also be used as paving material for pathways. If you decide to use urbanite to build a raised bed, however, be aware that it is usually 4–6" thick and can be cumbersome to climb over when reaching into a planting area. As mentioned before, wood offers the thinnest option for a raised bed, usually just 2" thick. Blocks take up a lot more room, so if growing space is at a premium in your yard, opt for something thinner. That said, if you are looking to make raised beds that appear earth-bound, solid, and hefty, urbanite or concrete blocks can create this look.

> **GEEKY GARDENING TIP**
>
> **A WORD ABOUT REDWOOD**
>
> Redwood is often sprayed with a solvent to aid the curing process. It takes a long time to dry redwood naturally, and milling companies have found that by spraying the wood with acetone or methanol, they are able to cure and dry redwood more quickly. While there is a process for removing the solvents after drying is complete, traces of these chemicals have been found in the wood, and can leach into the soil. Ask your lumberyard professional to verify whether the wood has been kiln- rather than solvent-dried.

Wooden posts and stones create a vegetable garden with Japanese overtones.

### Cinder Block

Cinder block, like urbanite, is a substantial building material for raised beds. Unlike concrete, though, cinder blocks are made with fly ash, a waste product of the coal industry. While there is no official study proving this, it is speculated that heavy metals present in fly ash—namely arsenic, cobalt, lead, and mercury—will off-gas and leach into groundwater and soil. Gardening forums have countless discussions on this subject, with healthy arguments both for and against the use of cinder block, but it deserves further investigation if you plan to use this material.

### Stones and Other Natural Materials

If you plan to grow mostly in-ground, but still want to include some decorative elements of design along with a few extra inches of garden soil, stones or other natural materials offer a lot of flexibility. No mortar is necessary unless you are building borders that are several layers high.

### Cob and Adobe

These earthen materials are used to build houses, retaining walls, and other structures. Both use a mixture of sand, clay, and straw to form whatever shape is desired. To make these structures durable as raised beds, and able to withstand constant moisture and soil contact, lime is added to a finishing plaster as a sealant. Alternatively, adobe bricks are often found in gardens designed using Permaculture principles and are an acceptable material for raised beds. Earthbags are another earth-based building material, often made from otherwise discarded, misprinted polypropylene bags. They simplify the building process: rather than making adobe bricks, you fill the earthbags with native soil (with as little as 5 percent clay) and stack them together. Earthbags can then be covered with a layer of adobe for a smooth finish. Some earthbag aficionados suggest coating the soil side of the new retaining wall with a layer of cement-based stucco plaster to help prevent degradation from excessive moisture.

## Guidelines for Shape and Size

When building your garden beds, there are several other things to take into consideration. Will you have small children in the garden with you? Do you want to bring a wheelbarrow right up to a raised bed? Do you have or anticipate having back problems? Are you a card-carrying neat freak? The answers to these questions will help you determine the size and shape of your beds, and how much space to leave between them.

### Just How Neat Are You?

Let's start with the last question first. The neat freak bit. It might not seem like a factor in gardening, but it can make the difference between spending time in the garden or not. If you prefer to have everything in its place, but you now have an unorganized random garden, you probably won't want to be there very often. A soldierly array of crisp raised beds might just be the ticket. Likewise, if you'd rather your vines ramble and you love the look of a lush, overgrown jungle, take this into consideration before installing formal, square beds. Chances are high a snaking border or keyhole garden is going to suit you better.

Your garden should match your needs. Do you want high production or do you just want to putter around? If you intend for this garden to produce a bounty of food for your family, you will benefit from structuring the garden with beds in full sun, and easy-to-access pathways with room for a wheelbarrow or large tubs. Build your planter beds wide enough to accommodate large plantings, but narrow enough to be able to access the produce without stepping into the beds. If, on the other hand, this garden is going to be a place to disappear and putter, then feel free to create cluster gardens, perhaps each with a different theme, and choose locations around your yard to tuck them in. Making choices that satisfy your needs will help you enjoy and use your garden more thoroughly. Let's look at some pointers for high-production gardens:

### Three Feet for Kids, More for Grown-Ups

An adult can reach the center of a raised bed from either edge most easily if the bed is no wider than 4'. It can be as long as you want—4', 6', 12', or more—as long as you can access the midline of the bed on the two long sides. Some bio-intensive methods call for beds that are 5' wide. In order to prevent soil compression that can occur while working these beds, farmers and gardeners usually keep a plank of wood on hand to distribute their weight evenly. They lay the plank down across the area and step or kneel on it instead of directly on the soil.

Children can't reach as far as adults, and will have to climb into your garden, disturbing the soil and possibly trampling seedlings if they can't reach the center. Limit kid-sized beds to 3' wide or less. A 3' bed will be sufficient for adults, while giving children room to grow. A 2' wide bed, while it may seem small, can be the perfect size for little hands in a school garden. While we're on the subject of kids, this is a good time to mention toddlers are usually pullers or diggers. They love to grab tiny seedlings and get a closer look. They like to dig tunnels to drive rubber duckies through to the other side. If this makes the hair on the back of your neck stand up, you might want to create a special garden just for the kids.

### Twelve Inches Deep

Unless you have rich, loamy, fecund soil to begin with, you will want to build a raised bed that is at least 12" deep. Adequate root space is critically important to a plant's health. Some gardening experts say 6" deep is plenty, but the truth is the deeper the soil is conditioned, the more easily plants will grow. Give your garden a good head start by building a foundation that is deep enough. For those using wood for this task, 2" × 12" lumber is best.

## Two-Foot Pathways (Three for Equipment)

An average gardener only needs 2' of space between beds in order to access the garden with ease. It is wide enough to kneel or sit down without backing into the bed behind you. If you plan to use a wheelbarrow or small garden cart, or need wheelchair access, make the pathways between beds at least 3' wide. Better yet, measure your cart/wheelchair and base your pathway dimensions on that. Some experts reduce the amount of space between beds in order to fit more crops. If you are comfortable with navigating the foliage that will inevitably spill out of your incredibly productive beds onto the pathway, feel free to reduce the pathways to 19" or less. Just be aware melons and squash will make for an interesting obstacle course.

Those are a few guidelines for high-production gardens. If you plan to have a more low-key, meandering garden instead, keep these principles in mind:

### Stepping Stones Are Your Friend

No matter how you set up your garden, it will be more easily managed if you place stepping stones in strategic places to help navigate around your growing areas. A well-placed piece of flagstone or tile can help direct wandering guests, and helps prevent soil compaction in conditioned beds. If you plan to have growing areas that are wider than 4', situate more stepping stones in the middle of the growing area to allow for ease of access.

### Mimic Nature

Nature presents itself in winding streams and spiraling vines. You can incorporate these elements of nature into the shape of your garden beds.

## GEEKY GARDENING TIP

### TRY A KEYHOLE GARDEN

A keyhole garden uses Permaculture design principles that aspire to create more edges in the garden. The more edges you create, the more planting surface you have. This design is based on the shape of a keyhole, and can be built as a waist-high raised bed or as low as a few inches above ground. Think of it as a circle with a pathway leading into the center from one edge. The circle is between 8–12' in diameter. The entire area of the circle is planted except for that pathway. Gardeners access the garden space from the center of the circle, along the pathway, and along the outer circumference of the circle. Some keyhole gardens incorporate a compost pile into the center of the circle. If you would like to try this, make sure your planting area is narrow enough to be reached entirely from the outside of the circle. Keyhole gardens are an efficient use of space and break the straight-line boundaries of formal raised beds.

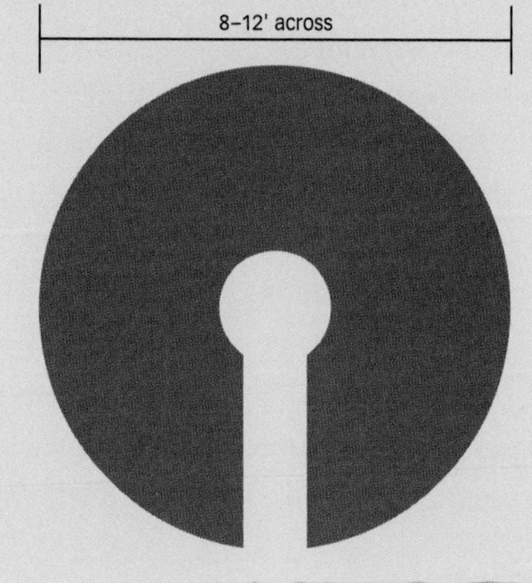

A curving pathway through irregularly shaped beds can be more inviting to curious guests than a bee-line entryway. You can also incorporate curves into the garden to capture water (more on that in the Irrigation chapter). If you plan to create undulating freeform shapes, it is much easier to use adobe or earthbags to build your raised beds than using wood. Bricks and stones offer similar flexibility. Just make sure your materials are not so thick and bulky that you lose access to the planting areas.

### Consider Where You Sit

There are many ways to create sitting spaces in the garden, and raised beds offer a couple of different ways to rest. You can create a sitting rail around the perimeter of the bed by adding a "cap" of a 2" × 4" piece of wood horizontally atop the frame of the bed. Secure the cap with 3" wood screws and add vertical supports—usually also made from 2 × 4s—that run top to bottom on the outside of the raised bed, underneath the cap. Another option is to place your raised beds closer together, with smaller pathways, so you can sit on the edge of one bed while working in the other. This strategy also helps those gardeners with lower back issues.

## HOW TO BUILD A RAISED BED

There are many ways to build a raised bed, from *Sunset Magazine*'s basic structure (*www.sunset.com/garden/perfect-raised-bed*) to less formal beds made from recycled fencing. Sunset's raised bed uses corner posts, but some gardeners prefer to reclaim those precious inches of growing space taken up by posts, and build their beds without them. Either way, if you build your bed with materials that last, using a few helpful tips offered here, you will be able to enjoy your raised beds for years to come.

- **Build on a level surface—**It seems like a no-brainer, but you'd be surprised how many people try to assemble their raised beds in the garden among the foliage. Do yourself a favor and build the beds on a concrete patio or other level surface, then move them into place.
- **Use deck screws—**It will save you time (and maybe even a trip to the emergency room) to use 3" galvanized deck screws or stainless steel screws

instead of nails. Predrill your holes if you are working with materials like Trex decking, which splits easily near the ends. A cordless hand drill will make this process go quickly.

- **Put the ugly side in**—Lumber has an ugly side. It always does. Whether it's a knot, a crack, or the neon orange spray paint the company used to mark the product, you are likely to find flaws in the wood. Be sure to situate that flawed surface to the inside of the raised bed, where the soil can cover it. While you're at it, check the wood for splinters or rough edges and point the roughest edge to the ground. This saves you time and effort later on, either pulling splinters out of your thumb, or sanding down your new bed.
- **Hardware cloth, not chicken wire**—If you have burrowing animals in your

## How to Build a Raised Bed

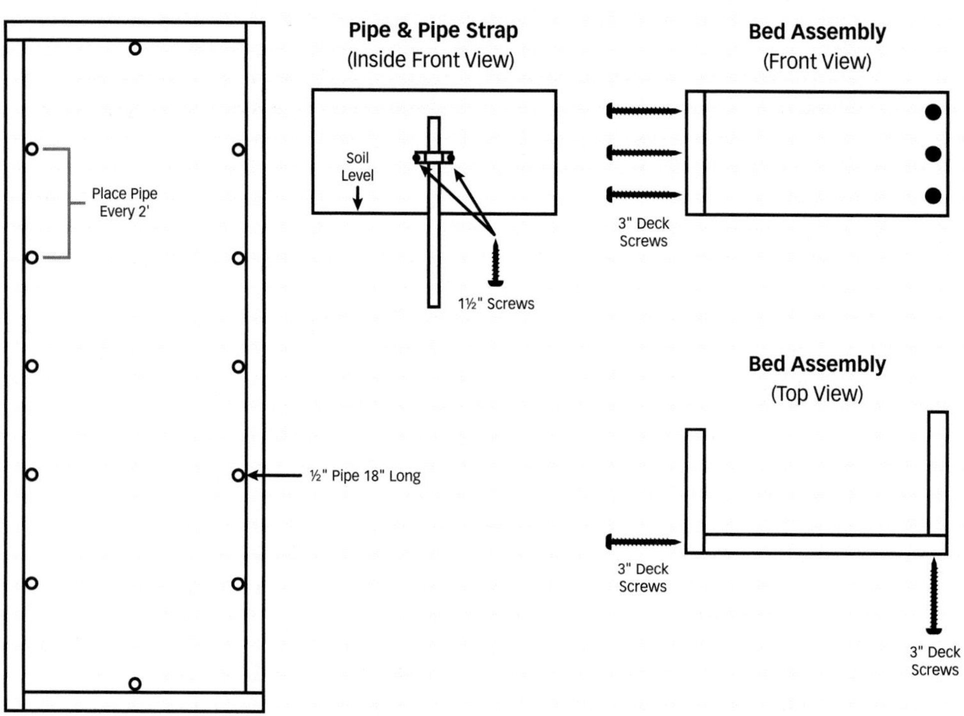


**Raised bed assembly.** Courtesy of Gardenerd.

neighborhood, there is one important step to take as you build your beds. Line the bottom securely with hardware cloth (welded wire mesh). Chicken wire is thin, and gophers can chew through it. Hardware cloth that's only ¼" or ½" will last for years and put your concerns to rest before you've even added soil to the beds.

## HOW TO BUILD A BED

1. Cut pieces of 2" × 12" lumber to the appropriate size. For a 4' × 8' raised bed, purchase three 8' pieces of lumber, and then you will only have to cut one board in half. Your beds will have an external dimension of 4' × 8', but your internal dimensions, the actual growing area, will be slightly smaller.
2. Align the pieces vertically and bring the corners together as shown (see the diagram) on a level surface. Predrill the holes as needed and connect the corners with three 3" deck screws per side.
3. Once the frame is assembled, flip the bed over and attach hardware cloth to the bottom edge (if you are using hardware cloth) with ½" construction staples. Return the bed to the right side and position it in the garden.
4. Check the bed with a level to ensure the foundation is . . . well, level. If your bed is sloped, water is likely to drain unevenly and you may experience pooling in low areas.
5. Next, use a mallet or hammer to insert the 18" lengths of ½" pipe against the inside walls of the raised bed. Place the pipes 2' apart. These prevent the wood from twisting or bowing under the weight of wet soil. It also prevents the bed from shifting over time, especially if you are building taller beds with several layers of wood. You will need to adjust the pipe length dimensions if you build taller beds. 18" pipe is appropriate for a 12" bed. Hammer the pipe into the ground so that the top end of the pipe sits about 1–2" below the top edge of the raised bed. You will not be able to see the pipes once the bed is filled with soil.
6. Secure each pipe to the wood frame with ½" pipe straps and two 1½"

wood screws as shown (see Pipe and Pipe Strap Inside Front View on the diagram). If you plan to attach a sitting rail or cap to the top edge of your raised bed, this is the time to do it.

7. Congratulations! Now you are ready to fill your bed with soil.
8. If you don't have enough existing soil and compost to fill your raised beds, you will need to start off with bagged nursery planting mix, bulk organic vegetable garden soil, or a combination of ingredients. Once the beds are established, regular composting will keep you supplied with soil amendments.

## Formula for New Raised Bed Soil

Before we get started, let's get something straight: there's no actual soil in potting soil. It's a misnomer. Potting soil is usually made up of some kind of decomposed organic matter, like compost, wood chips, lumberyard waste, and peat moss. It also has perlite—that white puffy stuff that looks and sounds like Styrofoam when you crush it. Perlite is puffed volcanic glass that allows water to flow better through the soil medium. It doesn't hold nutrients or add nourishment to the plants. It's simply there as a space holder for air and water.

Peat moss is widely used in potting soils to hold moisture and improve soil texture. It is acidic, and can help adjust alkaline pH when needed. The trouble is peat moss is a natural resource that is being depleted around the world. It takes about 3,000 years for nature to make a peat bog, and we're using it up faster than it can reproduce. As an alternative, some forward-thinking soil companies are starting to incorporate a peat moss substitute into their potting soils instead. That alternative is called coir. It's mispronounced by most, but the correct pronunciation of it (in English, anyway) is *coy-yer*. Coir works like peat to hold moisture and improve soil texture, but it's made from a waste product, so it's renewable. Coir is made from the outside hull of coconuts—the part that is thrown away. The raw product has a high salinity, so it must be thoroughly rinsed before use. Thankfully, most manufacturers producing coir for the hydroponics industry are meticulous in eliminating salts before packaging the product. Investigate your provider before using a new material, and inquire with your nursery professional about carrying coir-based products for your neighborhood.

That bag of potting soil from the store will probably say "organic" but know this: there is no regulation about the use of the word "organic" in soil amendments. When we go to the store and buy organic produce, we know it has been grown without pesticides and chemical fertilizers according to USDA organic standards. In the world of soil amendments, the word "organic" simply means "of, relating to, or derived from living matter." Keep this in mind as you read about fertilizers as well.

## Making Planting Mix

So now that you have an idea of what's in those bags, let's talk about how to make your own raised bed planting mix. Here's the formula: start with 50 percent compost, 40 percent coir, and 10 percent perlite or vermiculite, depending on your existing soil conditions. Vermiculite does the opposite of perlite. It is a puffed mineral that is exploded like popcorn. It holds water like a sponge, which helps sandy soils retain moisture. It doesn't break down, so you only need to apply it once. Vermiculite has a checkered past: at one point a major mining source became contaminated with asbestos, but OMRI (Organic Materials Review Institute) put regulations into practice to ensure each batch is now certified asbestos-free before sale.

You can also throw in coffee grounds and organic fertilizer if you like. This is just a starting point, however. If you mix in some of your existing soil, you will want to adjust the percentages a bit. If you have clay soil, add more compost to break up tight particles. If you have sandy soil, use more coir to hold moisture better. Play around with this. It's all part of the experiment of gardening.

Now to calculate your soil needs. If you have a raised bed that is 12" tall, it will be easy to figure out how much planting medium you will need. It's simply length × width × 1 = cubic feet (because your bed is 1' tall). If you have a shorter raised bed, you will need to do a little more math: length × width × height in fractions of feet. For example, let's say you have a bed that is 4' wide, 6' long, and 8" tall. First multiply 4 × 6 to get 24'. Then divide 12 (inches) into 8 to get 0.667. Multiply 24' by 0.667 to get 16 cubic feet of soil. If your bed is 10" tall, use 0.834; if it's 6" tall, use 0.5.

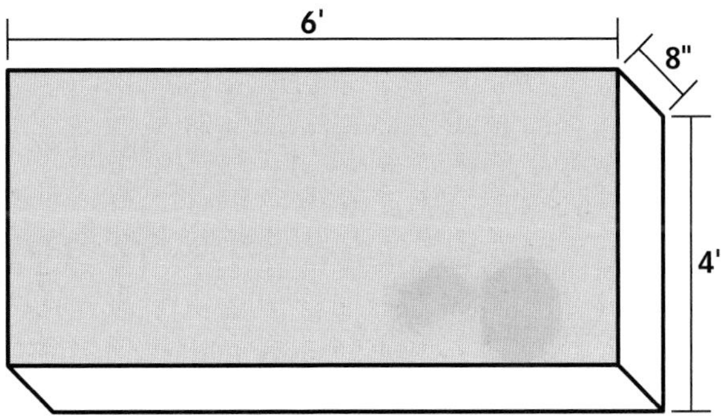


Volume = 4' × 6' × 8" (1"/12") = 16 cubic feet or 4' × 6' × .667 = 16 cubic feet

Once your cubic footage is figured out, multiply that total by 50 percent to find out how much compost you need. Then multiply the cubic footage total by 40 percent for how much coir, then by 10 percent for perlite. For example:

Our bed needs 16 cubic feet of soil.

50 percent of 16 is 8 cubic feet of compost.

40 percent of 16 is 6.4 cubic feet of coir, and

10 percent of 16 is 1.6 cubic feet of perlite.

Most bags of nursery potting soil and compost are sold in either 2 cubic feet or 1.5 cubic feet bags. Divide your totals for each material by the bag size you plan to buy and that will tell you how many bags to load into your car.

## Berm Beds

Often called unconstructed beds or mounds, berm beds are the right choice for those who want to build a garden without actually building anything, not even stacks of organic matter. These beds also allow for more creativity. They can be formed into any shape, length, and size to accommodate your grand garden vision. Do you want a snaking berm with sunflowers along the pathway, or a circle mound for your potato patch? Start digging.

There are several ways to build an unconstructed bed. A common practice is to mark out the bed areas (see the box about string lines) but instead of digging inside the bed area, dig soil out of the pathways and dump it onto the bed areas. This leaves the pathways lower than soil level and the beds higher than where they started. This technique was used by Native American cultures to irrigate their crops, and is often used in commercial agriculture today. The lower pathways fill with water, and the water is absorbed at the base of the mounds. Plant roots reach deeper for water, making them more resilient and drought-tolerant. In Permaculture, a variation of these pathways-turned-trenches is called a swale and is often used to divert water away from flood-prone areas toward plant root zones (we'll talk more about this in Chapter 7).

### GEEKY GARDENING TIP

#### OLD SCHOOL STRING LINES

When setting up mounded raised beds, place stakes at each corner of your target bed area and run string along the sides to map out clear lines for your beds. Whether you are building stacked mounds with layers of organic material, or just hilling up soil and compost, these lines will ensure your beds are straight.

Mounded beds have become extremely common. Turn to Appendix D for other ways to build mounded beds, including "no-dig" beds.

Mounded raised beds are usually between 4–8" tall, though some adventurous gardeners have been known to build them waist-high. Pathway soil is mixed with compost to create loamy, well-drained soil that will hold together in mounds. The sides are sloped and the surface of the mound is either flat across the top or has a gentle convex curve.

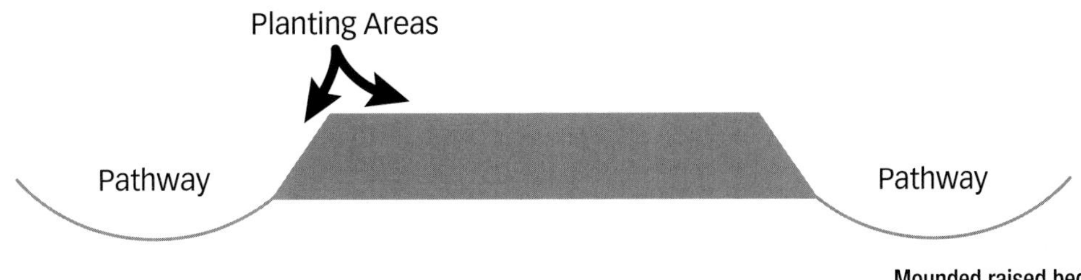


Mounded raised bed.

The theory behind this kind of mounded bed is that it creates more surface area. Sloped sides plus a flat top equals more soil exposed to the sun, which thaws and warms more quickly in spring. Some gardeners take advantage of the extra surface area by planting crops on the slopes of each bed. You gain up to another foot of growing space if your beds are 6" tall. Be aware that slopes can erode away during watering, so keep the slopes, if not the whole bed, well mulched to retain water and prevent soil loss.

## In-ground Planting

While unconstructed or berm beds are essentially the same as in-ground planting, the difference is height. An in-ground garden bed is made by loosening the existing soil of the desired planting area and working (digging) compost into the top 4–6". If you have existing soil that tends toward sand or loam, this is a fine choice. Those with clay soil will find it difficult to cultivate a garden this way without adding copious amounts of compost. In fact, clay soil is the reason raised beds were invented in the first place! Since clay soil doesn't drain well and takes longer to thaw after winter, use this method only if you have sandy, well-draining soil.

Be sure to test your soil before planting in the area. Most university agriculture departments offer basic soil tests, and some offer to test for heavy metals. Do you know the history of the land you plan to cultivate? With all these good intensions for healthier living, it would be a shame to inadvertently poison yourself by growing food in soil contaminated with heavy metals, so be safe and get that soil tested. We'll talk more about soil nutrients and heavy metals in Chapter 3. Conditioning an in-ground planter takes about as much sweat and elbow grease as an unconstructed bed. Many first-time gardeners like to try this method before committing to a formalized garden layout. It doesn't require a lot of planning, just a lot of compost. Work the compost down into the top 4–6" of soil. The deeper you loosen and amend the soil, the better your crops will grow. You can add decorative elements like stone or brick borders and put stepping stones throughout the planter to avoid compressing the soil.

No matter which type of raised bed you decide to use, just know that good planning pays off. Your garden will reward you with a bountiful harvest if you put some time and energy into the overall design and structure. Build your beds once and enjoy them for years to come.

# CHAPTER 3

# ALL ABOUT SOIL

Soil is the foundation of every great garden. Without healthy soil, plants may grow, but they won't thrive. Plants take up all of their nutrients from the soil (okay, plus the energy they get from the sun), and they need space to spread their roots, so it's important to create and maintain a healthy soil environment for your crops. What makes up a healthy soil environment? A lot of things. Let's take a look at the cast of characters.

## Nutrients

Soil contains a vast array of elements and minerals that play an important role in a plant's life. The Big Three are nitrogen (N), phosphorus (P), and potassium (K). Nitrogen is responsible for green, leafy growth. It's the thing that makes your tomato plants grow big, green, and bushy. Phosphorus helps those tomato plants develop strong roots, and more importantly, make flowers that eventually turn into fruit (yes, a tomato is technically a fruit). Potassium, sometimes referred to as potash, helps support a plant's overall vigor as well as fruit development and disease resistance. Together these three ingredients lend themselves to raising happy, productive vegetables.

The Big Three do not work alone, however. They have a supporting cast, an ensemble of minor characters helping to make their work easier. Trace minerals like calcium, sulfur, iron, magnesium, manganese, and boron all have jobs to do. They help facilitate nutrient uptake to plants, and perform specialized tasks like forming proteins, catalyzing chlorophyll, and dividing cells. The Big Three may be the stars, but they can't go on without the support of trace minerals.

## pH

Your soil will likely be acidic or alkaline, and soil pH measures the degree of that acidity or alkalinity. On the acid side of the soil spectrum (about 4.5), plants such as camellias, blueberries, azaleas, and hydrangeas thrive. In fact, the more acidic your soil is, the bluer your hydrangeas. On the alkaline side (about 8.0), artichokes, mint, and asparagus do well. Most vegetables like to grow in an environment that borders a neutral pH, which is 7.0, with many varieties flourishing in a range between 5.5–7.5.

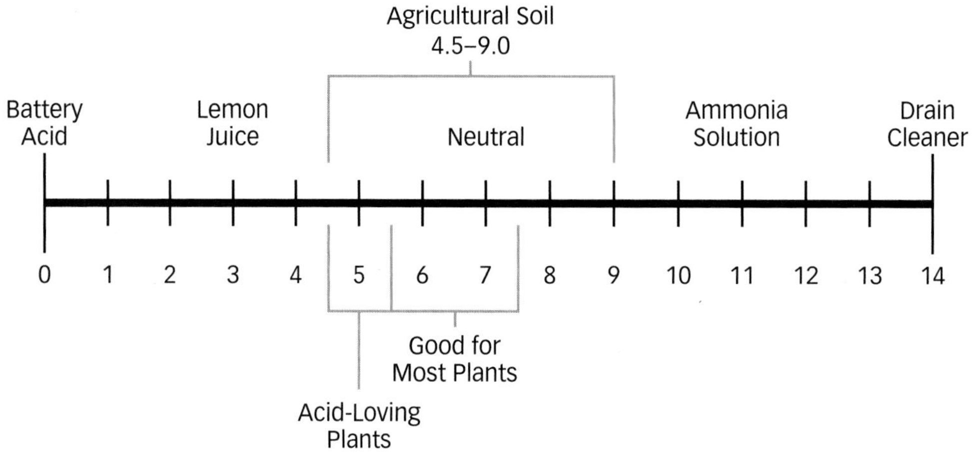


pH range for soil and common household items.

Changing the pH of your soil is not like changing the pH of your swimming pool. In a pool or spa, you just add a few chemicals and *poof*, the pH is different. It doesn't work that way with soil. It can take years to alter the pH of your garden soil, so the best approach is to find plants that do well in your existing soil conditions. That said, we'll cover ways to amend your soil to increase acidity or alkalinity later in this chapter.

## Soil Texture

It's time for a very important question: When you stick a shovel in the ground, does it slide right in, or does it barely penetrate the soil? Your soil's texture is going to determine how hard you will have to work to get your garden ready for planting, or at least which type of planter bed you will use. With texture, there is also a spectrum, just as with the acid/alkaline spectrum: your soil texture will fall somewhere along the spectrum between clay, silt, and sand. There are pros and cons for each.

Microscopically, clay soil is made up of small particles, with very little airflow between them. Clay soil tends to drain poorly and is difficult to dig. In spring, in places where the ground freezes over, clay soil takes much longer to thaw, drain, and become ready to work than sandy soil does. Many gardeners avoid the whole process by building raised beds (turn back to Chapter 2 if you decide you want to do that). The benefit of clay soil is it holds water and nutrients very well. Gardeners don't need to add fertilizer as often, nor do they need to water as much. So it isn't all bad.

Sandy soil, on the other hand, is very loosely put together. Unlike clay soil, which forms into hard clods that are difficult to break up, sandy soil runs through your fingers and doesn't hold together if you try to form a clump. Under a microscope, you can see it is made up of large particles. It's fantastically easy to dig, and drains very well. The problem is it drains too well. As a result, sandy soil loses moisture quickly, and with all that fantastic drainage away flows all of your carefully applied nutrients as well. Gardeners with sandy soil have to water more frequently and generally have to stay on top of adding amendments.

Silty soil behaves like a combination of clay and sand. The particles are larger than clay, but nowhere near as large as sand. These particles characteristically feel silky, smooth like flour or some even say greasy. Silty soil has a tendency to become compacted like clay, making drainage and digging difficult. Silt and sand are both made up of weathered rock particles, so they both respond to gravity in the same way—the particles will settle quickly in a water solution.

# SOIL FOODWEB

In addition to soil nutrients and micronutrients, there is an entire world (or underworld, in this case) of insects and microbial life forms in your soil that make the plant-world go 'round. It's called the Soil Foodweb: fungi, bacteria, protozoa, earthworms, and nematodes all have a purpose—a job to do. They are the backstage hands making the show run flawlessly.

Dr. Elaine Ingham, a soil microbiologist, first wrote about and coined the phrase Soil Foodweb during her research on soil microbiology in the 1980s and '90s. Jeff Lowenfels and Wayne Lewis, while tipping their hats to Dr. Ingham, uncover this world in their book, *Teaming with Microbes*. They deftly explain how plants not only take up nutrients, but also "produce chemicals they excrete through their roots." The excretions, or "exudates," are then consumed by fungi and bacteria, which in turn are consumed by protozoa and nematodes, which then excrete waste that is taken back up by the plant as food. How convenient! Don't forget the host of arthropods and insects, which burrow and aerate the soil, living and completing their life cycle (naturally or otherwise—being eaten by birds or other predators). When they die, their bodies go back into the food chain, breaking down into usable organic matter, which is once again consumed by microbes, and eventually plants. This overlapping series of complicated food chains is the Soil Foodweb. It's fascinating stuff, but why does this matter to you as a gardener?

It matters because when your soil is healthy enough to support this intricate underworld of microbial activity, your garden will be more likely to thrive. Not only that, but everything you do in the garden can help or hamper the Soil Foodweb. Every box of fertilizer, every shovelful of compost, every bottle of bug spray that is used on your plants affects this underworld. Don't worry, though, I'll give you all the information you need to know to steward the microbial life in your garden's Soil Foodweb later in this chapter.

## Get Tested

The first thing to do, before adding any fertilizers or soil amendments, is to get your soil tested. It takes a little time, and you have to wait for the results, but it's worth it. There are two kinds of tests available: basic and complete. Basic soil tests reveal the nutrient levels of your Big Three. These tests usually require that you take a soil sample, mix it with water, and let it settle. Then you draw off some of the liquid and add it to a beaker with specific chemicals that are reactive to nitrogen, phosphorus, or potassium (this is the fun science part). Close the container, shake it, then leave it undisturbed and wait for the color to change. The results are compared against a color chart to let you know how well supplied your soil is with that particular nutrient. You can buy basic soil tests for N, P, K, and pH at many nurseries or order them online through gardening catalogs.

The second type of soil test yields more elaborate results. A complete test involves sending a soil sample away to a laboratory. Soil technicians not only provide you with N, P, K, and pH ratings, but also trace elements, salinity, and heavy metals. Why is this important? Well, let's say you live in a city near a busy road. Your test might show high levels of zinc in the soil. Where did that zinc come from? Zinc disperses from braking systems on vehicles, from roads, from airplanes overhead, and from galvanized metal gardening tools (like watering cans or buckets). Excessive zinc prevents the uptake of nutrients in plants. That's right; it actually blocks the plant's ability to extract N, P, and K from the soil. A soil test might also show the pH of your excessively zinc-laden soil is acidic. This would tell you if you were to raise your soil pH, you would bind up the zinc, making more nutrients available to your plants.

It's always a good idea to get a complete soil test to rule out the presence of lead (residues from turn-of-the-century oil drilling, leaded gasoline, and house paints), arsenic (previously used near railroads as a weed killer for years), mercury, cadmium, or aluminum. Most university departments of agriculture offer inexpensive soil tests (just search the Internet for "university soil test" to find one near you), or you can send a sample to soil labs like Wallace Laboratories (*www.wlabs.com*) in El Segundo, California, or Timberleaf in Murietta, California (*www.timberleafsoiltesting.com*).

## Make Amends

Once you know the nutrient levels of your soil, you can amend accordingly. Soil amendments—also called inputs—can increase available nutrients, but also can alter soil texture or improve drainage. Let's revisit your soil texture—clay, silt, and sand. What can be done to improve these conditions?

Surprisingly, the organic solution to hard-packed clay soil, compacted silt, and loose, anemic sandy soil is one thing: compost. In clay and silty soil, compost serves to create space between particles and allow more airflow, which then helps the soils drain better. In sandy soil, compost works as a sponge to retain moisture and provide structure to hold nutrients. Compost brings these extreme conditions closer to the perfect texture for growing vegetables and fruits. This ideal is called *loam*. Loamy soil holds nutrients but drains well. It supports the easy proliferation of root systems and is nearly effortless to dig. Loam is the goal that every gardener hopes to attain with soil.

So how much compost should you apply to your soil? The general rule of thumb is to add compost in inches. Add a ½–1" layer at the beginning of each season before planting, and if needed, again during mid-season to boost production. You can either top-dress, meaning spread it out on the surface and leave it, or you can work it into the top few inches of soil. Soil Foodweb aficionados prefer to apply compost on the surface, without disturbing the delicate strands of fungal hyphae and microbial life hard at work in the soil. The microbes will utilize the compost as it filters through the soil during regular watering and as larger insects and earthworms till it into the soil for you. All of this activity makes nutrients available to plants with less work from you.

Gardeners with very sandy soil may choose to ignore the ½–1" rule of thumb, and add compost with reckless abandon. It's okay. Add compost, then add more compost, and when you think you've added enough, add more. Your soil will be just about right at that point.

In addition to benefiting soil texture and structure, compost adds nitrogen and inoculates your soil with those backstage hands we talked about earlier. Compost does much more than feed the soil; it brings it to life with fungi, bacteria, microscopic insects, and earthworms. It supercharges your soil with the microbiology needed to help plants thrive. You can buy bagged compost from nurseries, but why not make it yourself? It's a great way to recycle nutrients in your garden and cut down on waste

that goes to the landfill. Best of all, making your own compost means you know exactly what's in it and you don't have to drive anywhere to get it.

## Start a Compost Bin

A compost bin can be any structure that holds garden biomass (use this term instead of "waste," because you're not wasting anything). A compost bin can be a cylinder of hardware cloth, an old trash can with the bottom removed and holes punched in the sides, or an official store-bought plastic compost bin. You don't even need a bin, *per se,* to store your compost. You can make a pile in your backyard and let it cook. The important thing is to start using your own garden biomass to give back to your garden. Here are a few guidelines for creating a viable composting system:

- **Size:** The ideal minimum size for a compost bin is 3' × 3' × 3'. That is the magic size at which organic mass begins to generate and hold heat.
- **Space:** Allow enough space for your compost bin or pile, plus enough space right next to it for another pile. Why? At some point you will want to "turn" the pile (to aerate it and expose new surface area to all of those microbes that will continue to break down the organic matter—that makes the pile heat up again), so ideally you can use that space next to your compost pile to flip a pile from one side to the other without exerting much effort.
- **Browns and Greens:** Composting is a chemical reaction between carbon (usually brown-colored biomass) and nitrogen (often, but not always, green-colored biomass). Carbon-rich materials like dried leaves, wood chips, dead cornstalks, wheat chaff, and cardboard are combined with nitrogen-rich materials like kitchen scraps, coffee grounds, grass clippings, cover crops (like fava beans, alfalfa, and bell beans), and garden trimmings to start the process. See the Appendix for an expanded list of browns and greens.
- **Other Ingredients:** Compost requires moisture in order to break down brown and green biomass. Water is a key ingredient. In climates with regular rainfall, you may never need to water your compost pile once it's built. In fact, some

gardeners have to cover their compost pile with a tarp to keep it from getting too wet (excess moisture promotes anaerobic bacteria—the kind that stink). But in dry climates, you will need to water your pile regularly. Start by thoroughly watering each layer of the pile as you build it. If you use alfalfa or straw, it will take a lot of water to wet the material completely. Be patient and don't be afraid to use plenty of water. According to Alane O'Rielly Weber, a certified Soil Foodweb advisor at Botanical Arts in San Mateo, California, you should be able to squeeze a drop of water out of a handful of biomass. If not, it's not wet enough. A helpful tip to use as a guideline for moisture: your pile should be wet like a wrung-out sponge. Water begins the process of biodegradation and invites beneficial microbes to feast upon the decaying matter, so it's a really important ingredient in your pile.

- **Soil:** This is another key ingredient, and it is often omitted from many composting guides. You don't need to buy those silly boxes of "compost starter"; use soil instead! Healthy soil inoculates your compost pile with fungi, bacteria, and microorganisms, which go to work to break down organic matter, to aerate the pile as they crawl through, and to digest material. The result is high-powered, high-vitality compost that improves your soil with every application.
- **Layers:** Composting guides vary and will tell you the ratio of brown material to green material ranges anywhere between one part brown and two parts green, to five parts brown and one part green. It can get confusing. Keep it simple. Use inches instead of parts or volume measurements. Put down a 2–3" layer of browns, then a 2–3" layer of greens, a shovelful of soil, and water it in. Repeat this process until you have used up your ingredients.

## Geek Alert: Active Batch Thermal Composting

If you want to get more technical and build an amazing compost pile, try this method for Active Batch Thermal Composting. Wait a minute. What the heck does that mean?

- **Active**—you are turning the pile and monitoring temperatures
- **Batch**—you are building the whole pile all at once rather than adding materials over time
- **Thermal**—it gets hot, up to 160°F with the right materials
- **Composting**—you are breaking down garden biomass into black gold

Active Batch Thermal Compost Pile.

Okay, now the method.

Figure out how much material your compost bin will hold in gallons. Then gather your browns and greens in 5-gallon buckets using this ratio that Dr. Ingham recommends for beneficial bacterial-dominated compost, which is great for vegetable gardens:

- 35 percent high-carbon/brown materials like wood chips, sawdust, dried leaves;
- 45 percent nitrogen/green materials like chipped tree and garden trimmings, coffee grounds, and grass clippings; and
- 20 percent high-nitrogen biomass like alfalfa, legume cover crops like fava beans, or manures. These high-nitrogen materials kick up the heat quickly and provide food for the bacteria to feast upon.

Multiply the number of gallons your compost bin holds by each percentage. That will tell you how many gallons of each type of biomass you will need. Then divide each number by 5 (if you are using 5-gallon buckets) and that will tell you how many buckets of each material you will need. For example, if you have a 50-gallon compost bin, you will need 17.5 gallons, or 3.5 buckets of browns; 22.5 gallons, or 4.5 buckets of greens; and 10 gallons, or two buckets, of high-nitrogen/legume/manure materials. With Active Batch Thermal Composting, you don't have to use layers, since you are building the pile all at once. You do need to mix the materials together as you put them in the bin, though, and water the pile the entire time. Check the temperature between eighteen to twenty-four hours after building the pile and it should be hot. When it gets

## GEEKY GARDENING TIP

### KEEPING CRITTERS AWAY FROM COMPOST

Always end your composting layers with brown material on top. It keeps fruit flies and odors—and the vermin who love odors—away. To add more kitchen waste, pull back the top layer of browns, add your scraps, and then redistribute the brown material on top.

to 160°F, it's time to turn the pile. Each time the pile is turned it will heat up again (remember, new surface area will be exposed, giving microbes more food to consume). Turn the pile again after temperatures peak. Eventually the pile will cool down and within three to four months you will have microbe-rich compost for your garden. If you don't have enough material to build a pile all at once, that's okay. Building a pile over time is still considered composting. Your pile will just take longer to process, and won't get as hot.

## Fertilizers: Chemical, Organic, or None?

When it comes to fertilizers, there are three roads to take: use chemical fertilizers, use organic fertilizers, or don't use any fertilizers at all. It's an argument that's been going on since the mid-1950s between farmers who use conventional growing methods and those who farm organically. Permaculturists and some bio-intensive farmers would argue that nature provides its own fertilizer, so we don't need to add any inputs.

It's easy to be enticed by all of the options on the nursery shelves. Those boxes of fertilizer offer the promise of quick-fix solutions and gigantic, succulent vegetables. Some of them prove helpful, while others can cause long-term damage. Before you pour anything onto your soil, it's important to know what fertilizers do and why you might need them.

First, let's step back in history a little bit. Around the turn of the nineteenth century, farmers used one of two methods to fertilize their croplands.

Method 1: They tilled in manure from farm animals or acquired copious amounts of horse manure from what was then known as the transportation department (think mounted police here). Farms were different then, they grew more than just one crop, and there were always plenty of animals around to contribute to fertilization.

Method 2: Farmers infused their land with nitrogen by growing a cover crop of legumes such as fava beans or peas. The fields were seeded with bean seeds, and after the crops had grown tall, farmers

cut them down and dug the biomass into the soil. The biomass decomposed and improved the soil structure, but the magic was happening underground in the roots.

The air we breathe is 76 percent nitrogen. Legume crops have the ability to pull atmospheric nitrogen out of the air and lock it into the plants' roots. Here's how it works: friendly bacteria called rhizobia (part of the Soil Foodweb) establish a home in the roots of leguminous plants. The bacteria are able to "fix" nitrogen in the root, in the form of little pink nodules. When bean plants just begin to flower, the roots are full of these pink nodules. The crops are strategically cut down and the roots are left in the soil to biodegrade, a process that eventually releases the fixed nitrogen into the soil. A farmer would then plant crops and enjoy the benefits of amply supplied nitrogen.

A third, unpredictable way to fix nitrogen into the soil as fertilizer was to hope for lightning. Lightning deposits hundreds of thousands of pounds of nitrogen into soil every year. It happens when the energy of lightning breaks the bonds of nitrogen molecules in the air. The particles mix with vapor and rain, fall to the earth, and are absorbed into plants and soil. This method is helpful but not enough to supply the full amount of fertilizer needed for most farmers.

Along came German chemists Fritz Haber and Carl Bosch, who figured out how to manufacture synthetic nitrogen. They did this in the early twentieth century by combining atmospheric nitrogen and hydrogen to create ammonia (widely used as ammonium nitrate in fertilizers today). The technique, the Haber-Bosch Process, was lauded as one of the most important inventions of the day, and gave the farming community tools to solve world hunger. The German duo won Nobel prizes for chemistry in 1918 and 1931.

Despite the promise of increased yields, history has uncovered several issues with synthetic nitrogen. First of all, synthetic nitrogen is made from natural gas. Natural gas is a common source of hydrogen, and while that's perfect for the Haber-Bosch Process, it's a natural resource and the supply is finite. Strike one against synthetic nitrogen: it is not sustainable.

## How Much Nitrogen?

The next thing to consider is how much nitrogen, synthetic or otherwise, is actually taken up by plants. Much like humans, who absorb nutrients in minute quantities over time, plants only take up a small amount of nitrogen, in much lower doses than synthetic brands of fertilizer provide. A box on the nursery shelf might list the Big Three (N, P, K) ratios like 20–20–20 or 30–30–30. Those are very high numbers when it comes to fertilizer.

Think about this: What happens when you take a multivitamin? Your body absorbs some of it, but what happens to the rest? It flushes away. The same is true for plants. What isn't absorbed by the plant is released down into the water table. Once there, it travels out to sea through waterways. Rivers and bays with excess nitrates develop algae blooms because, remember, nitrogen is responsible for green, leafy growth. Algae are hungry for oxygen, and rob the water and fish of that life-giving resource. The result is a dead zone. Strike two against synthetic nitrogen.

The third strike is a serious one. Nitrates are very high in salts. High salinity diminishes a plant's ability to take up water, which causes stress and stunted growth and can eventually kill a plant. Arguments have been made, even by reputable soil scientists, that plants can't tell the difference between organic and synthetic nitrogen. That may be true, the plants may not be able to tell the difference . . . but your soil can. High-salinity, high-nitrate fertilizer kills soil microbes. It burns them or causes them to flee. It destroys your Soil Foodweb. Okay, maybe strong soil biology will survive the onslaught, but it will still take a hit. If you worked hard to create your ecosystem both above and below ground, to create an environment where nature does much of the work for you, take a moment to consider what synthetic fertilizers do to the soil before you apply them.

## The Benefits of Organic Fertilizers

Now let's talk about organic fertilizers. These amendments range from plant-based materials like alfalfa, to minerals like rock phosphate, to animal by-products such as bone meal. Each has its own properties, and typically several nutrients are combined to create "balanced" fertilizers for different plant groups. On nursery shelves you will find a box for vegetables, one for roses, another for acid-loving plants, and yet another for fruit trees. Each company has a proprietary blend it feels is best for its customers. The blend of nutrients appears on the box as the ratio of our Big Three, and those numbers will range between three and seven—much lower than synthetics. For example, a box of organic citrus fertilizer may list a ratio

of 7–4–2, meaning the total content of each nutrient is 7 percent nitrogen, 4 percent phosphorus, and 2 percent potassium.

With numbers that low, the nutrients are more likely to be taken up by plants in total, leaving little behind to infiltrate the water table. Still, any fertilizer should be used with caution; more is not necessarily better. Let's take a look at available nutrient options.

### Nitrogen: Green Leafy Growth

Animal-based sources of nitrogen include blood meal, feather meal, hoof and horn meal, and fish meal. They generally have a rate of 9–15 percent in pure form. Both hoof/horn and fish meal also contain some percentage of phosphorus, fish meal being higher. Blood and feather meal may have little to no phosphorus, depending on its source.

Nonanimal-based sources of nitrogen are alfalfa meal, cottonseed meal, soybean meal, and kelp meal. These fertilizers offer a lower rate than their animal-based counterparts, between 1–7 percent. Another great source of nitrogen can be found in your coffee maker. Spent coffee grounds supply nitrogen at a rate of about 2 percent, with trace levels of phosphorus and potassium. Compost is a source as well, but it may surprise you that compost is relatively low in nitrogen. However, as we discussed earlier, plants take up nutrients in small amounts, so the available nitrogen is sufficient in many cases. Plus, with the bonus of the vibrant, nutrient-building microbial life forms that compost provides, it makes a fantastic fertilizer.

Animal manures, which straddle the categories above—being *from* animals but not a by-product of slaughter—are higher in nitrogen when dried, according to North Carolina State University research. Dried cow, chicken, and hog manures and fresh rabbit manure all provide nitrogen at a rate between 1–2.2 percent.

### Phosphorus: Roots, Fruits, and Flowers

Bone meal is the predominant animal-based source of phosphorus, but as mentioned above, many of the animal-based nitrogen fertilizers also supply some phosphorus. Bone meal supplies a rate ranging from 11–22 percent.

Rock phosphate and soft rock phosphate are nonanimal sources of phosphorus. They are both mined from sedimentary rock, rock phosphate as tri-calcium phosphate, and soft rock phosphate as a by-product of the mining industry. They supply 2–3 percent phosphorus.

In the manure category, seabird or bat guano (a nice way of saying poop) is excellent. These resources range from 10–15 percent phosphorus, and also have between 1–3 percent nitrogen.

### Potassium: Overall Vigor and Fruit and Flower Development

Animal-based fertilizers supply virtually zero potassium, so we'll skip right to nonanimal-based options. Sulfate of potash, also known by the commercial name SulPoMag (meaning sulfate of potassium-magnesia), is the most common source of potassium. Potassium remains in the soil for years, so make sure you test your soil first before applying. It may not be needed. Other options include greensand, which supplies between 3–7 percent potash. It is marine sediment mined from ocean-adjacent rock formations. If you have very sandy soil, avoid greensand, because it will make soil texture even sandier. Kelp meal and liquid kelp emulsions generally supply low levels of potassium but offer the benefit of trace minerals as well. Wood ashes, depending on what is burned to create the ash, can provide small amounts of potassium and phosphorus. Don't use wood ashes if you have highly alkaline soil, since it tends to raise pH.

Animal manures, both in dried and manure tea forms, supply potassium as well as the other nutrients above. Like liquid kelp emulsions, animal manure and manure teas also supply a broad spectrum of trace minerals.

Remember, as mentioned earlier, that even if that box of fertilizer says "organic," it doesn't mean the source of that bone meal or manure was raised organically. It just means it's derived from organic matter and that it is safe for use in organic agriculture.

### pH Adjusters and Trace Minerals

Trace minerals play a role in nutrient uptake, and depending on geographic location and farm practices, these minerals can become depleted. As mentioned above, some organic fertilizers supply a small amount of trace minerals. That may be all you ever need to use. But you might be wondering what all of those other boxes on the nursery shelves are for. It's important to know what they are and what they do before applying them to your garden. Oftentimes, products that provide trace minerals also serve as soil pH adjusters. They will raise or lower your pH, and sometimes this is a good thing. Sometimes, not so much.

Limestone and dolomitic lime both raise soil pH, but calcitic or high-calcium lime, not surprisingly, supplies calcium as well. Dolomitic lime adds calcium and magnesium. For soils that have plenty of magnesium, it is recommended to use calcitic lime instead of dolomitic lime.

Gypsum is often used to break up clay soils, and contains calcium and sulfur in moderate amounts. The sulfur in gypsum also lowers pH. If you have soil pH that is already lower than 5.8, do not use gypsum.

The trouble with many soil and pH modifiers is sometimes they solve one problem while creating another. Gypsum is the perfect example. It can lower the soil pH, making unwanted heavy metals like zinc more available to plants (remember, excessive zinc blocks nutrient uptake). Gypsum can also raise the salinity of soil, tipping the balance and disrupting soil microbial life. Limestones add minerals but raise pH, which alkaline soils don't need. Investigate these soil modifiers thoroughly and get a soil test to be certain you need these trace minerals before adding them.

The one exception just might be glacial rock dust. It's another soil modifier that has been touted as the solution to every soil issue in recent years. Even purist Permaculture experts and devout biodynamic practitioners hail the stuff as a wonder-amendment. It is a by-product of the quarry industry, and comes mostly from the process of cutting and polishing granite. It remineralizes depleted soils with a broad spectrum of trace minerals like calcium, magnesium, iron, and micronutrients. It does not significantly modify soil pH, but it is typically alkaline. What's more, beneficial soil microbes like it too, and worms find it handy to have around—they ingest it as grit in order to process food. Farmers and home gardeners have seen dramatic increases in production by amending the soil with glacial rock dust.

## Seek Out Worm Castings

Also known as the other "black gold," worm castings prove that big things come in small packages. Worms ingest your kitchen scraps and garden waste, and then leave behind castings (another nice way of saying poop). Those castings are full of nutrients and can be used to fertilize your garden plants. Be aware that a little bit goes a long way. Jeff Lowenfels shared this statistical information about worm castings in *Teaming with Microbes:* "They have ten times the available potash; five times the nitrogen; three times the usable magnesium; and they are one and a half times higher in calcium . . . than soil that has not been through an earthworm." There's another component to worm castings that makes them a superior fertilizer. Let's dive into the science.

Worms don't have teeth. They have enzymatic mouthparts instead. The enzyme they use to break down food is called chitinase (pronounced KY-ti-nās). Chitinase also breaks down chitin, which happens to be an important component of insect

exoskeletons. Chitinase is excreted in worm castings, and when you fertilize your plants with castings, the plants take up the chitinase enzyme. When pests nibble or suck on the now chitinase-laced plants, they start to wonder why they're falling apart—they're eating an enzyme that dissolves their exoskeleton! So worm castings aren't just a great fertilizer; they solve pest problems like whitefly and mealy bug, too.

Having a worm bin not only helps produce your own castings for fertilizer and pest control, but it gets rid of kitchen scraps, too. A worm can consume half its body weight in food scraps every day. So if you have 1 pound of worms in a bin, you can safely assume your worms will be able to put away ½ pound of food scraps each day. That's about 3½ pounds per week. Sure, you can buy the bagged stuff at the nurseries, but the way to know for certain that you have viable, microbially active, enzymatic-rich castings is to make them yourself, just like compost. The benefit of having less food waste is a bonus. For instructions on how to make a worm bin, see Start a Worm Bin in Chapter 4.

To apply any of these fertilizers, follow suggested amounts and directions on the packaging. Use the appropriate amount to prevent runoff, and keep an eye on your plants to see how they respond. Whichever of these fertilizers and soil modifiers you decide to use in your garden, mix them well into the soil before planting. Plant roots prefer not to come in direct contact with fertilizers, so avoid throwing a handful in a planting hole and plopping down your transplant unprotected. Mix amendments so they are well blended, then plant your veggies and seeds. If you decided to add these amendments to the soil surface after planting, mix them first with compost, spread them among your plants, and scratch them into the top few inches of soil.

As you can see, soil is a big subject with plenty of nuance. Now that you have an understanding of what's going on in your underground ecosystem, it's time to move on to strategic planning in the garden.

# CHAPTER 4

# PLANNING YOUR GARDEN SEASON

It's a ritual that happens every year. Seed catalogs begin to appear in mailboxes, graph paper and pencils come out from hiding, and dreams of bountiful harvests propel gardeners forward into the growing season once again. There are so many seed varieties to try; how and where will they all fit in the garden? When should you plant? And what the heck is crop rotation? This chapter will help you figure out your growing season or seasons, as well as what to plant in each. It will also give you some helpful tips to ensure the continued health of your garden and soil.

## Find Your Frost Dates

Nature has a way of putting an end to summer gardens. It's called frost. Most climates have a first and a last frost. The phrase used to express the range of time when planting is either safe or unsafe is called "frost dates." When you don't have a frost (think warm-winter climates like Los Angeles) the concept of frost dates has little or no meaning. For everyone else, it's life or death in the garden. Knowing your frost dates helps ensure success each growing season. Here's a basic primer:

- **First Frost**—the day everyone dreads in fall. It means the end of the gardening season for most unprotected gardens. That frost comes through and wipes out most plants (some can survive with protective garden fabric covers, and some even thrive after a frost—e.g., kale and parsnips become sweeter). Most first frost dates occur between September and November in the northern hemisphere (March through early June in the southern hemisphere).
- **Killing Frost**—consists of a drop in temperature to the point that freezes water. The cells of plants are full of water and when water freezes it expands. When water in cells expands, it ruptures the cell, essentially killing the plant. Not every frost is a killing frost. In fact, some climates make it through winter with only a light frost.
- **Last Frost**—the day everyone awaits in spring. It's the reported average date after which a killing frost is not likely to occur. Most seed packets bear instructions saying "start seeds indoors six to eight weeks prior to last frost." That way, plants are ready to go in the ground once the threat of frost has passed. Last frost dates usually fall between March and May in the northern hemisphere (August to September in the southern hemisphere).

To find your frost dates, you can ask your local university agriculture department or a neighbor who has been gardening for a few years. There are online resources to look up your frost dates by zip code. The first is the National Climatic Data Center (*www.cdo.ncdc.noaa.gov*), which allows you to choose by state and scroll down to find your city. The document lists spring and fall frost dates with probability ratios that decrease as the season progresses. For example, Aliceville, Alabama, has a 90 percent chance of spring frost around March 28, but a 50 percent chance of frost around April 10, and only a 10 percent chance by April 24. It would be safe to assume that planting after April 24 is okay, and your plants might be okay if you planted them after April 10. It's a 50–50 chance. If you want to take the risk, use insulated garden

fabric to protect crops and your plants will most likely be fine.

Another website offers gardeners a simpler view of frost dates by simply typing in your zip code. Dave's Garden, a longtime favorite resource of many home gardeners, uses the National Climatic Data Center's database, but summarizes the information by county to make it a little more digestible: *www.davesgarden.com/guides/freeze-frost-dates/*. Either website allows you to geek out, learning more about your frost dates.

**Above: Cool season crops.**
**Below: Warm/hot season crops.**

## What to Plant Each Season

This is the fun part. Once you know your frost dates, you will know whether you have one growing season or more. Climates that experience killing frosts generally plant crops from spring through fall, and shut down the garden for winter. Those who have a greenhouse or other protected environment for crops can learn to surmount the challenges of winter gardening. Warm-winter climates that get light or no frost can grow year-round.

So, take a look at your growing season and figure out how many frost-free days you'll have to work with. From there, decide what you want to grow.

### Cool Season Crops

In most climates, these are vegetables that prefer to grow in early spring, before summer's heat kicks in. Seed packets for these veggies will often say, "Start six to eight weeks prior to last frost." How long your cool season lasts depends on those frost dates. In warm-winter climates, these crops can also be planted in spring, but they tend to do better if planted in late summer or early fall. They will thrive over winter until it's time to plant warm weather crops in spring.

### Warm Season Crops

As spring temperatures rise, some plants prefer warmer soil and sun exposure to thrive, or even to germinate. These are good transition crops as the season progresses.

### Hot Season Crops

These are the quintessential summer favorites most gardeners look forward to growing each year. They typically require warm soil to germinate and higher temperatures to set fruit.

Here is a list of cool season crops.

### Cool Season Crops (*start indoors or buy transplants)

Arugula
Beets
Broccoli*
Brussels sprouts*
Cabbage*
Carrots
Cauliflower
Celery
Chard
Collards
Cover crops
Fava beans (direct sow)
Garlic (direct sow cloves)
Grains—quinoa, spring wheat, rye, amaranth
Green onions
Herbs—all but basil
Kale
Kohlrabi*
Leeks
Lettuce
Mesclun Mix
Mustard greens
Onions
Parsnips
Peas—sugar snap and snow
Potatoes (from sprouted potatoes)
Potatoes (sow pieces with eyes)
Radishes
Rutabagas
Shallots
Spinach
Turnips

The cool season is also a great time to plant strawberries, fruit trees, artichokes, and asparagus crowns. Warm-winter climates can plant those in fall.

Late fall or winter is the time to plant bare-root fruit trees, roses, and cane berries. These crops will work to develop roots over winter and will then be able to focus on top growth when spring temperatures arrive.

Warm and hot season crops grow best from late spring through early fall. Plants should be well established before scorching temperatures set in, as some varieties won't set fruit if temperatures are over 90°F. The flowers will drop off instead. Plan accordingly to make sure you have room for these summer sizzlers.

Here is a list of warm/hot season crops.

### GEEKY GARDENING TIP

#### FIND YOUR HARDINESS ZONE

Like knowing your frost dates, having a handle on your hardiness zone will help you choose plants that thrive in your climate. The USDA produces and updates a nationwide map that shows what the minimum average temperature is for your zone. It is standard practice for nursery catalogs to publish hardiness zone ranges for the plants they sell. Visit *www.arborday.org/treeinfo/zonelookup.cfm* and type in your zip code to find your hardiness zone. Once you know which zone you're in, you can order plants from catalogs that are suitable for your zone. Nurseries should already carry plants adapted to your growing area. Knowing your zone will also help you identify plants that need special growing conditions if grown outside their hardiness zone range.

### Warm/Hot Season Crops (*indicates hot weather crops)

Basil
Bush/pole beans*
Corn
Cucumbers* (start indoors—or plant starts later)
Eggplant*
Lettuce (direct sow or transplant with protection in hot weather)
Lima beans*
Muskmelons
Okra*
Peppers* (start indoors—or plant starts later)
Summer squash* (zucchini, yellow crookneck, etc.)
Sweet potatoes (from slips)
Tomatoes* (start indoors from seed—or plant starts later)
Watermelon*
Winter squash* (pumpkin, acorn, butternut, etc.)

## Keep the Family Together

As we discussed in Chapter 1, plant placement is all about strategy. You can plant tall crops to the north and shorter crops to the south to ensure everybody is getting the sunlight they need. You can strategize to plant tall crops in front of short crops to provide some shade for cool weather vegetables as they mature in warmer weather. These are great tools to have in your pocket (along with the slide rule and pocket protector), but there are a couple of other things to keep in mind as you plan out your garden.

Plants have families, or rather, they belong to families. When you plot out the location for each crop, it's a good idea to keep these families together. Why? Because some plant families take up certain nutrients from the soil and others can leave behind diseases that can later be picked up by another member of the family that is planted in the same place year after year. See where we're going with this? By planting vegetables in the same family together, you will be able to track where that family has been planted, and where it can be planted next year and the year after. Gardeners have good memories, but there's no need to tax the system (a.k.a. your brain) too much by planting a broccoli here, a broccoli there, a broccoli everywhere. Since those broccoli are in danger if they are planted back in the same soil within three years, it's much easier to move a plant family to a new location if you keep plants in that family grouped together in the first place. Let's look at some of the families in the vegetable kingdom. Common names have been used here to introduce them.

- **Cole crops** (*Brassicaceae*)—often called brassicas, this family includes broccoli, cauliflower, cabbage, Brussels sprouts, kohlrabi, and kale. It also includes turnips, radishes, and mustard greens. If you need a hint to keep it straight, they all form bright little yellow flowers when they go to seed.
- **Nightshades** (*Solanaceae*)—vegetables in this family include tomatoes, peppers, eggplant, and potatoes. Tobacco is also part of this family—think of it as the black sheep.
- **Alliums** (*Amaryllidaceae*)—the ever-popular onion family includes leeks, onions, garlic, shallots, and chives.
- **Squash** (*Cucurbitaceae*)—Cucurbits, as plants in this family are often called, include cucumbers, melons, winter and summer squash, watermelons, and gourds. By the way, summer squash grows in the summer; winter squash does too. The name refers not to when it is grown, but when it needs to be consumed and how long it stores. Summer squashes such as zucchini and yellow crookneck

have thin skins that can easily be pierced with a thumbnail, so they have to be eaten shortly after picking. Winter squashes like pumpkin and butternut have a thick skin that cannot be pierced with a thumbnail, so they can be stored over winter, thus the name winter squash.

- **Carrot** (*Apiaceae* or *Umbelliferae*)—every plant in this family is an umbel, which means when it goes to seed, it forms an umbrella-shaped flower. Dill, parsley, cilantro, fennel, celery, carrots, and parsnips all belong to this family.
- **Beet** (*Amaranthaceae* or *Chenopodiaceae*)—Do you like quinoa? Never heard of it? It's part of the beet family along with beets, chard, spinach, Orach mountain spinach, and mangels. The two families mentioned in parentheses were merged, so now amaranth is also included. Plants in this family tend to extract lead from soils, so if you've tested positive for high amounts of lead in your soil, lay low on the beets et al.
- **Bean/Pea** (*Fabaceae/Leguminosae*)—chili wouldn't be the same without the members of this family, which include peas, lentils, beans, fava beans, a host of other dry beans, and peanuts. These crops, when cut down in the flowering stage, leave behind nitrogen for the next round of plants to feed upon. This family is an important part of sustainable gardening practices.

Plant these families together to make crop rotation easier down the line.

## Crop Rotation for Healthy Soil

There are a number of reasons to rotate crops in a healthy garden. As mentioned above, different crops pull different nutrients (or different levels of nutrients) out of the soil, and can leave behind diseases or even pests. By planting a broad selection of vegetables, fruits, and herbs in your garden, and rotating those crops each season to a different spot, the likelihood of diseases, pests, and soil depletion is much less.

Unlike farmers who grow acres and acres of one crop, also known as monocultures, you have the opportunity to garden sustainably with biodiversity. Biodiversity means simply a variety of life forms in your garden—much like our ecosystem of Chapter 1. A greater diversity of plants helps decrease the chances of future disease and pest infestations. Biodiversity also eliminates monoculture's main problem—taxing the soil beyond its capabilities. It's the opposite of putting all your eggs in one basket. That's smart gardening.

Another reason to rotate crops is to close the loop on inputs. Strategic crop rotation can help put nutrients back into the soil after one crop pulls them out. Here's how: some crops are heavy feeders, meaning they consume a lot of nutrients in order to grow and produce fruit. Other crops give back to the soil, replenishing nitrogen and breaking down into beneficial organic matter that helps rebuild soil structure or provides biomass for the compost pile. Plants that fix nitrogen are heavy givers. By rotating heavy feeders with heavy givers, you will greatly reduce the amount of fertilizer and other inputs needed to garden sustainably.

John Jeavons of Ecology Action has spearheaded forty years of research on sustainable agriculture. In his book, *How to Grow More Vegetables*, he discusses the importance of crop rotation for nutrient recycling. "For many years Ecology Action often followed a heavy giver, heavy feeder, light feeder, low nitrogen lover type of crop rotation approach," Jeavons writes. Now they use a simpler approach of planting cover crops (heavy givers) followed by heavy feeders, followed by a legume crop that is grown to maturity. When legumes are grown to the point they form beans or peas, all the nitrogen that has been stored in the plant during early growth is transferred to the beans. So the plant doesn't technically pull nitrogen from the soil, it uses its own resource. Jeavons calls this period of the rotation the "soil nitrogen resting" phase. While there appears to be a difference of opinion about which plants are heavy or light feeders, here are some examples of each:

- **Heavy Feeders**—tomatoes, corn, eggplant, Brussels sprouts, and squash
- **Light Feeders**—Swiss chard, sweet potatoes, leeks, carrots, and parsnips
- **Heavy Givers** (if cut down during flower stage)—fava beans, alfalfa, peas, and clover
- **Legume Crops for Nitrogen Resting**—most bean and pea varieties

However you decide to rotate your crops, choose a diversity of plants to include in your garden. The rewards will be paid out over years in successful harvests.

# START A WORM BIN

If you don't have enough room in your garden for a compost bin, consider starting a worm bin to reduce waste and provide high-powered fertilizer for your plants. Worm castings contain concentrated nutrition for plants as well as microbes and chitinase (see Chapter 3 for more details).

Worm bins come in all shapes and sizes. Prices range from a few dollars for a basic plastic tub to over a hundred dollars for an easy-to-use upward-migrating system. If you are just getting started, and don't want to spend a lot of money, start with a single chamber plastic bin.

It's easiest to start with a heavy-duty plastic storage bin, like Rubbermaid, that is around 20–24" long, about 16" wide, and between 8–12" tall. Your container should have a lid that snaps on and completely covers the bin. This will prevent water from dripping into the bin during wet weather. Water in the bin leads to drowning accidents. Worms rarely survive such adventures, so keep a lid on it and all will be well.

**A Rubbermaid plastic bin with holes drilled across the top.**

Your bin requires air holes. Some gardeners prefer to drill ½"–1" holes with a paddle bit along the top edge of the container walls (see photo at left), others like to drill tiny holes (less than ¼") along the bottom. Holes on the bottom may allow worms to escape, but they allow leachate or worm tea to drain away. If you choose to drill holes in the bottom, stack the worm bin inside a second bin without holes in order to catch the leachate. This will prevent drowning accidents as well.

To make bedding for a single chamber worm bin, use shredded newspaper, shredded office paper or cardboard, or coir. Many worm bin kits come with a coir brick. Soak the brick until it expands and absorbs water, and then layer it on the bottom of the bin. Some gardeners like to soak shredded newspaper in water, while others soak fist-sized cardboard pieces instead and mix those with dry shredded newspaper. Mix shredded paper with shredded newspaper (torn into long strips) to keep the texture of the bedding consistent throughout. Put down a layer of bedding several inches thick for your worms.

Once you have installed your bedding, it's time for food scraps. Lift up some bedding from one corner of the bin and place some kitchen scraps. Worms like most foods, but there are a few guidelines: no onions, no citrus, and no meat or dairy. Leave out oily foods, and cut up your scraps as small as you can. Worms have to wait for food to begin decomposing before they can eat it. The smaller food scraps are, the more quickly they will break down. Cover the food scraps with the bedding you pulled away, and then cover the entire surface of bedding with a moist sheet of newspaper. Put the lid on and check regularly, adding food scraps to a different corner each time.

Upward-migrating worm bins are sometimes called worm condos, and are fancier domiciles for your worms. There are usually two or three trays that stack on top of each other. The lowest tray is the oldest, and the newest tray is on top with a lid. Each worm bin manufacturer will have specific instructions for preparing the bedding—some use sheets of cardboard on the bottom, others use coir, still others use shredded newspaper with cardboard on top. When you get one of these bins, start by preparing one tray with food scraps and bedding. As the worms consume the scraps and the tray fills with castings, you simply add another tray with food scraps and bedding above it. The worms will migrate up to the next layer, leaving your bottom tray virtually worm free and ready for harvesting. This feature gives upward-migrating bins an advantage over single chamber bins.

In a single bin, when you want to harvest worm castings you can do one of two things.

1. Move the entire contents of bedding over to one half of the bin. Add a thick layer of new bedding and some food scraps to the cleared side and wait about two weeks for the worms to migrate to the new area before harvesting the castings from the old side.
2. If you don't have the patience for this technique, dump the entire contents of the bin onto a tarp and make little piles of castings. Worms hate light so they will burrow to the bottom of each pile. Wear a headlamp to intensify the light, but work in a shady spot out of direct sunlight. Scoop castings off the top of each pile until you have separated the worms from your castings. You will need to combine piles after a while. Return the clump of worms to the bin and deliver the castings to your garden.

A word about storage: shade! Worms hate light and heat. They will die or leave home if you give them inhospitable living conditions. Keep the bin in full shade or in a garage.

## Companion Planting

When plotting out your garden, the next thing to consider is who to put next to whom. Companion planting is an age-old practice of grouping together plants that get along well, and separating them from plants that don't. Do plants really care? Apparently they do. There are plenty of studies that debunk companion planting, but just as many that support it. With all the controversy, why not take it with a grain of salt, but use the principles of companion planting to your advantage. You may see some benefits.

Louise Riotte first wrote about companion planting in *Carrots Love Tomatoes: Secrets of Companion Planting for Successful Gardening* in 1975. Her book sits on the shelves of thousands of gardeners who crack it open each year during spring planning. Rodale Press also published their version of a companion planting guide, *Companion Planting Made Easy*, in 1995 as part of a series of publications on *Successful Organic Gardening*. It's available on the *Organic Gardening Magazine* website if you're willing to give up your email address. Both texts corroborate the partnerships we'll discuss here, but this just skims the surface of the pond. If you really want to geek out and dive into companion planting lore, check out those books. Here are a couple of examples of good companions, as well as kids who don't play well together.

### Favorable Partnerships

- Cole crops like onions, potatoes, and celery.
- Beet family crops like onions, lettuce, and cabbage.
- Bean/pea crops like cucumbers. Pole beans help corn (think Three Sisters Gardens).
- Cucumbers like beans and peas right back.

There is such a web of favorable companion connections; it's hard to keep it straight, especially when you add in what plants don't like.

### Unsavory Connections

- Cole crops don't care for strawberries or tomatoes.
- Beet family crops don't get along with pole beans.
- Bean/pea crops dislike members of the onion family.
- Cucumbers and other squash family members dislike potatoes.
- Oh, and fennel—everyone hates fennel. Plant that in a corner away from your other crops.

So why do some plants get along while others don't? Let's look at some of the reasoning behind it using some of the examples above.

Pole beans and corn have a mutually beneficial relationship because corn is a heavy feeder and pole beans fix nitrogen into the soil. Meanwhile, corn reportedly decreases the presence of leafhoppers that attack bean plants. Beans and peas dislike onions (is it the bad breath?), but onions help most other crops grow well because their odor repels insects. Some sources say to keep beans away from peppers because they are both susceptible to anthracnose. Likewise, tomatoes and corn should be planted away from each other because the tomato fruitworm and the corn earworm are one and the same pest. Tomatoes and potatoes, both members of the *Solanaceae* family, are best kept apart because they are susceptible to blight, which can spread easily from one to the other. But wait, aren't we supposed to keep plant families together? You can see how this companion planting business can get confusing.

When planning your garden, keep a trusted set of books, including one on companion planting, close by (see the Bibliography and Resources section). Rather than memorize all of these plant combinations and aversions, it's much easier to flip through a book to confirm a hunch. Over time you'll start to remember which plants are friends or foes, and you will be able to experiment with plant combinations to see what works in your garden.

## What's in Your Pencil Case?

When you get right down to it, gardening takes planning. Now that you have the guidelines for laying out a successful garden, it's time to put it all down on paper. Yes, paper. It may sound old school, but nothing anchors an idea better than writing it down. The act of putting pen, or in this case pencil, to paper is a creative process like any art form. Here's what you'll need.

### Space

It may be your kitchen table or desk, but you might need more room than that to spread out all of your seed catalogs and packets. Hint: floors and beds make great workspaces. Lay everything out in visual range so you can reference them as needed. Speaking of . . .

## Catalogs and Seed Packets

You may have a collection of seeds that each need a place in the garden this season. The best way to know what you need to plant is to have those seeds close by. While you're at it, check to make sure you have enough of each variety. The catalogs are there to inspire and replenish supplies. Garden geeks typically have pages dog-eared, hopeful they will have a place for a new variety or two. Group your seeds by plant family. It will come in handy when it's time to plot out crop locations.

## Graph Paper or Template

Graph paper makes it easy to define raised beds, rows, or square feet. Instead, you may prefer to print up a blank template of your garden beds on your computer each season. If you don't plan on changing the shape of your garden each year, this might be the way to go.

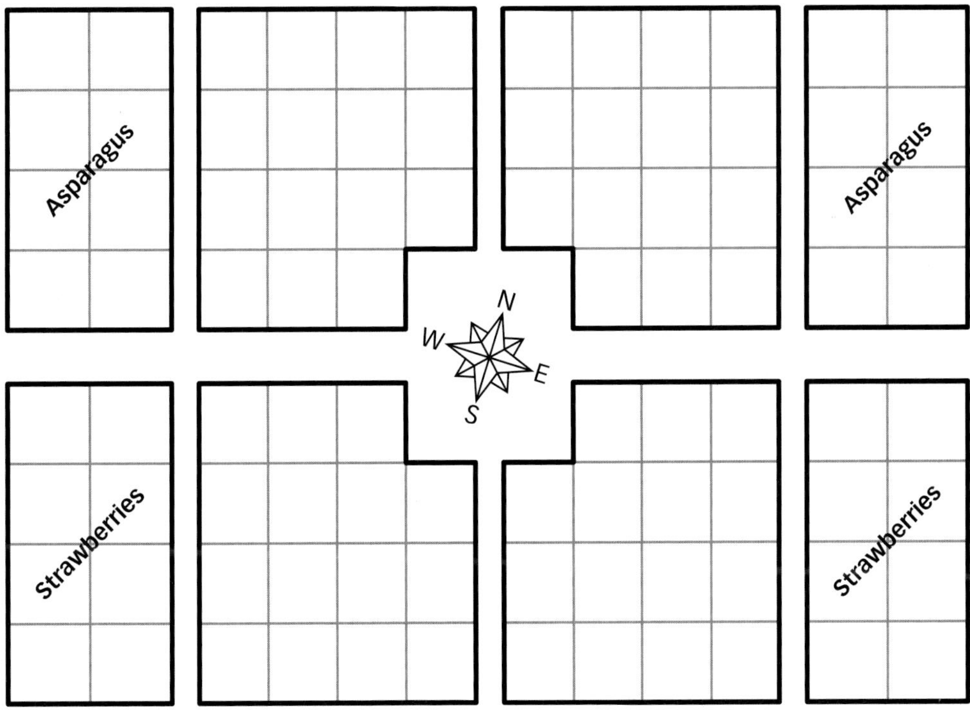

### Pencil and Eraser

Planning a garden is like completing a crossword puzzle. With all the different things to consider—companion planting, crop rotation, height and sprawl—you're bound to make a guess/mistake or two. Go for the mechanical pencil; it has a fine point for writing in small spaces. Skip the puny pencil-end eraser. You'll want the big guns for this, a white vinyl drafting eraser.

### Ruler

A straightedge of some kind is always helpful when drawing garden beds or measuring out square feet. If you don't have a ruler, use a notepad with cardboard backing or any other straightedge in the house.

### Gardening Books

Keep *Gardening for Geeks* close by (of course) as well as books on companion planting and bio-intensive gardening methods (we'll cover those in the next chapter). Once you're solid on the crops that work in your climate, you may not need to refer to your books as often.

### Put It All Together

Draw your garden space, raised beds, planters, etc., and then indicate where north is, relative to the beds. Now you're ready to plug in plant varieties in each bed. Start with tall and trellised crops, placing those to the north of the garden or each bed. Document your crops from last season, which may keep growing a few months more, such as garlic or Swiss chard. Keep plant families together as you fill in your beds on paper. Consult companion planting books for partners in crime. As you assign vegetable locations, move corresponding seed packets out of view, so you know what still needs a space. Make note of which seeds to order and refill. Put the seeds you won't be planting out of view. When you're done, you will have a fully planted plot of land on paper, with perhaps a few empty spaces for whatever tickles your fancy later on. Congratulations. You're ready to start seeds, prep garden beds, and plant for the season.

# CHAPTER 5

# SMALL SPACE/URBAN GARDENING

Unless you live in the wide-open spaces of sun-soaked farmland, chances are you have a limited amount of space available for gardening. Urban gardening has grown in popularity (no pun intended) over the past few years, and more than ever people are looking for ways to maximize their farmable land. Small space gardening techniques help you get the most out of your gardening space, whether you have acres or just a balcony.

## Bio-Intensive Methods

"Bio-intensive" is an umbrella term used to describe different gardening methods that help you grow high volumes of produce in small spaces. This chapter will give a brief overview of four bio-intensive methods that accomplish the task. Some of them focus on true sustainability, incorporating techniques that replenish topsoil, recycle biomass, and build self-sufficient communities. Even if you can't incorporate all of these techniques in total, you can implement some and set a goal for others.

## Consider Biodynamics

In Chapter 1, we explored the idea that our garden has its own ecosystem, by including beneficial flowers, bat houses, and toad abodes. Biodynamics goes a step farther and treats the farm or garden itself as a living organism. The principles of biodynamics were founded by Rudolf Steiner (1861–1925) in Europe in the early 1920s. Steiner believed in much more than soil microbiology and the marvel of transpiration in plants. He believed the living organism of a farm goes beyond the boundaries of the farm's fence. It includes the cycle of seasons, and beyond that, even the lunar cycle and other cycles of our solar system. It might sound hokey to some, but there are plenty of successful biodynamic farms, vineyards, and orchards that can attest to the benefits of considering these concepts. Biodynamics, at its core, is about creating a sustainable organism (your garden) that is as close to self-reliant as possible.

The folks at Demeter Association, Inc., the institution that certifies biodynamic farms, have summarized the concept perfectly by saying, "An important social value of biodynamic farming is that it does not depend on the mining of the earth's natural resource base but instead emphasizes contributing to it."

So how does a biodynamic farm work? For starters, it strives to integrate crops and livestock together. Animal manures are wonderful high-nitrogen fertilizers. Farmers use the manures from livestock to feed the crops. The crops feed the livestock in return. It's a closed-loop system. Of course, humans are in there somewhere, helping to facilitate the cycle from animals to crops and back. We are also eating the results. You might be asking, "But how does livestock work in a small space situation?" Let's look at that.

### Biodynamic Livestock

While it's not for everyone, if you have room for a few chickens, you have a resource for animal manure to feed to your compost bin. The compost in turn feeds your garden. Chickens also eat grubs from the compost bin and bugs from the garden. If your garden isn't large enough for chickens or livestock of any kind, then look to a friend who might—expand that ecosystem to include neighbors with horses, goats, or even rabbits.

As mentioned above, biodynamics also uses the lunar calendar to determine favorable days for planting, harvesting, and starting seeds. *Stella Natura* (*www.stellanatura.com*), the yearly publication that tracks the phases of the moon and its subsequent gravitational pull, is the tool by which most biodynamic farmers live and plant. There is science to support this stuff. In a ten-year study, Dr. Frank A. Brown showed that plants absorbed more water during full moons. Other research has shown seeds germinate more quickly if planted two days before the new moon. Whether you believe in it or not, the idea behind biodynamics is to use all environmental observations (and influences) to create a healthy, productive, and sustainable operation.

Along with sustainable practices, biodynamics encourages the use of Preparations (numbered 500–508) to inoculate compost piles, strengthen

**GEEKY GARDENING TIP**

**THE SCIENCE OF COMPOSTING**

Here are some Bunsen burner details for the uber-geeks out there: A study was conducted at Washington State University's Department of Soil Sciences using compost piles of cow manure and wood shavings. Biodynamic Preparations were applied to some of the piles, but not to the control piles. The same amount of water was used in each pile. After eight weeks of active composting, "Biodynamic-treated composts maintained an average 3.4°C higher temperature . . . suggesting more thermophilic microbial activity and/or faster development of compost with BD treatment . . . At the final sampling, BD-treated piles respired $CO_2$ at a 10% lower rate and had a larger ratio of dehydrogenase enzyme activity to $CO_2$ production . . . Final samples of BD-treated compost also had 65% more nitrate than control piles. Biodynamic Preparations thus effected discernible change in compost chemical and microbial parameters." How's that for an ecosystem!

microbial life, and prevent diseases. These Preparations include key herbs like valerian, stinging nettles, chamomile, and yarrow. They are grown on the farm and fermented into a compost-like consistency or liquid that is then combined with or sprayed onto compost piles.

You may be wondering how all of this applies to small spaces. Hold tight, it will all become clear shortly. For now, just remember the key points about biodynamics: farm as living organism, integration of crops and livestock, and recycling of nutrients (composting).

## What Is French Intensive?

Prior to the twentieth century just outside of Paris, farmers grew food using a method that conserved space and resources. They recycled horse manure from the transportation department and turned it into fecund soil that yielded plentiful crops—far more than traditional row farms produced. They carried the manure in baskets that were worn like backpacks, with long boards extending overhead to keep tall mounds of manure from falling onto their heads. Like biodynamics, French intensive gardening had its own set of principles that governed the way land was cultivated and crops were raised.

### 24" Deep

French intensive farmers conditioned their soil to a depth of 24" using a technique called double digging. By preparing the soil to that depth, plants develop stronger and deeper root systems, allowing them to pull nutrients and minerals from otherwise inaccessible soils below.

Garlic planted bio-intensively.

## Raised Beds

These were not necessarily traditional wooden raised beds, although vintage photos have shown those in use. Typically, mounded raised beds were a result of double digging. After working in compost or manure to condition the soil, the beds were naturally elevated. Farmers were careful not to step on the beds once prepared. Beds/mounds were usually 5' wide, but could be as long as 100'.

## Hexagonal Planting

Also known as offset rows or diagonal planting, this method of planting allows farmers to grow more seedlings in each bed. The plants are set in offset rows rather than in traditional rows.

What does hexagonal planting look like? Let's say you have a sheet of chicken wire. Lay it down on the soil and place a bean seed in the center of each hole in the wire. Then lift up the chicken wire. Each seed will be equidistant from every other seed on all sides. Your first row of seeds will be a straight line across the top. Your second row of seeds will start below the first, exactly halfway between the first and second seed of the first row. What are the benefits of hexagonal planting? There are many.

1. By planting hexagonally, plants are closer together than they would be in traditional rows, which means you can fit more into the same amount of space.
2. As plants grow, their shoulders touch, creating a living mulch. This eliminates sun and heat, greatly reducing weeds and evaporation of precious water.
3. Just like the penguins at the South Pole huddling together for warmth, plants grown hexagonally create a microclimate for themselves, which supports healthy crops. Young plants were often protected by individual cloches, glass bells, to create a mini greenhouse for each plant. See Chapter 9 to learn how to make your own.

## Succession Planting

French intensive farmers planted their beds over time, rather than all at once, to maintain a steady harvest throughout the season. If you love lettuce but don't want twenty heads of romaine all at once, you can do what these farmers did. Plant a 1–2' section of a raised bed with lettuce seeds or transplants (hexagonally, of course) on day one. On day fourteen, plant another 2'. Do that until you run out of space for lettuce and you'll never run out of lettuce. As another type of succession planting, farmers also planted short-season crops immediately following long-season crops in order to have something growing in the garden at all times.

These techniques can be applied to small spaces in order to get the most out of your garden. Let's look at how these two techniques were combined to form a new bio-intensive growing method that is used by millions today.

## DOUBLE DIGGING

Double digging is often thought of as back-breaking work, and it can be. It is the practice of conditioning the soil to a depth of 24" using compost, a shovel, and a digging fork. It is highly recommended to improve clay soils when establishing new garden beds. Whether to continue double digging each year is a point of debate.

- To begin double digging, mark out the planting area. It could be 4' wide and 25' long, or any variation you desire. GROW BIOINTENSIVE, which we'll talk about in a minute, works with beds that are 100 square feet, so 4' × 25' is ideal if you plan to implement that method.
- Put down a 1" layer of compost across the entire surface of the bed.
- Starting at one end of the bed, use the shovel to dig a trench 12" wide and 12" deep. Move the soil from that trench into a bucket for later use.
- Optional (use if you have very heavy/clay soil) Add another 1" of compost to the bottom of the trench.
- Use the digging fork to loosen the soil at the bottom of the trench to a depth

of 12", working the compost (if using) into the cracks as you do. Congrats, you've finished your first trench.

- Now dig a second trench, removing the next 12" of soil. Dump that soil into the first trench.
- Continue adding compost and loosening the lower 12", and repeat the process with each trench.
- When you get to the end of your bed, fill the last trench with the bucket of soil from your first trench. Celebrate with a hot soak afterward.

## GROW BIOINTENSIVE (Mini-Farming)

Alan Chadwick, an Englishman born in 1909, is credited for taking the key principles of Biodynamics and French intensive methods and combining them into something new. He mentored with Steiner and, some forty years later in 1967, started the UC Santa Cruz Garden Project. He developed an agricultural technique that combined double digging and hexagonal planting from French intensive with farm-as-living-organism, the lunar calendar, and the integration of crops and livestock from biodynamics.

John Jeavons furthered Chadwick's work with another forty years of research to develop what is now widely known as GROW BIOINTENSIVE or Mini-farming. His research is published in *How to Grow More Vegetables*. The basis for Jeavons's research came from the realization that our planet is losing farmable land due to soil erosion and desertification caused by unsustainable farming practices and destruction of rainforests. For every pound of conventionally grown food we consume, Jeavons says between six and twenty-four pounds of viable topsoil are lost. Organic farming is better, but still not sustainable. For every pound of organically grown food we consume, three to five pounds of viable topsoil are lost.

Corn, beans, and asparagus planted bio-intensively in raised beds.

We currently require between 7,000–63,000 square feet of land per person (less for basic survival, more for extravagant living) to grow every bit of food, and materials for clothing, fuel, and shelter. Our population is growing, leaving less land per person. Jeavons's research shows we can count on having fewer than 9,000 square feet of viable farmland per person in the near future to fulfill our essential needs. If that's the outlook of the future, then logically we would need to be as efficient as possible with our land, right?

Jeavons set out to find a way to use less land while creating a system that affords people with few or no resources—water, fertilizer, land, and money—a sustainable way to grow high-calorie crops and a means to earn income. GROW BIOINTENSIVE was born, using double digging, hexagonal planting, recycling of nutrients, and more, to reduce the amount of land needed per person to only 4,000 square feet.

Whether you have 4,000 or 400 square feet to work with, you can apply these practices for a more sustainable garden. There are a few key components to GROW BIOINTENSIVE worth noting. We've already covered double digging for soil conditioning, and hexagonal planting for efficient plant spacing, but let's look at another important principle to consider. It's a magic formula for sustainability: 60:30:10. What does it mean?

## 60 Percent

Remember how we talked about inputs and having to go to the nursery to buy bagged soil and fertilizer for the garden? What if you never had to do that? What if you were able to grow enough nitrogen- and carbon-rich material on your land so that at the end of the season, you were able to cut it all down and put it in your compost bin, and a few months later, you would have enough high-quality compost to feed your garden and rejuvenate those beds? That would be great. That would be a closed-loop system. These nitrogen- and carbon-rich materials are called "carbon and calorie crops." Corn and other grains such as wheat, rye, barley, millet, quinoa, amaranth, and oats are all great sources of biomass for the compost bin, but they also give you a harvest before cutting down the material. Fava beans are also on the list. These crops serve the dual purpose of providing calories and biomass.

So what's this 60 percent all about? Think of it as a goal. It may take a while to attain it, but if you can dedicate 60 percent of your garden to growing these "carbon and calorie crops," you will have enough material to generate enough compost to feed your garden all year, without trips to the nursery. If 60 percent sounds like too much, start with 25 percent—one raised bed out of four each season. You'll see the difference it makes in the quality of compost and your wallet.

### 30 Percent

If you lived in a country where food was scarce and land was precious, it would be advantageous to grow crops that provide the highest calorie content per square foot as possible. Crops like potatoes, parsnips, and sweet potatoes provide a lot of calories, but more importantly they provide higher yields (calories included) per square foot. The 30 percent part of the equation is relegated to these crops. If you can dedicate 30 percent of your land to growing high-calorie crops, you can feed your family more substantially with less land.

### 10 Percent

The remaining 10 percent is for all the crops you love to grow like tomatoes, peppers, squash, lettuces, and carrots. It might sound a little depressing to think such a small amount of land is dedicated to the crops we're used to growing, but in truth, those other crops aren't wasted either. They help provide sustenance for your family and food for your compost bin.

A GROW BIOINTENSIVE garden might have corn and quinoa growing in the spring/summer followed by fava beans or another cover crop over winter. It might also have potatoes and sunflowers (grown for the nutritious seeds and biomass), parsnips, and Jerusalem artichokes—another 30 percent crop. Then there might be a section of broccoli, carrots, lettuces, and peas. It doesn't sound too far off from a traditional garden. The difference is these crops are planted hexagonally in deeply conditioned soil, using companion planting and crop rotation, and the compost made from the biomass is going to feed the garden more effectively, instead of eroding soil away with conventional methods.

There is much, much more to the GROW BIOINTENSIVE method, and if you are interested in learning more, check out *How to Grow More Vegetables* or the abridged, kinder-gentler publication by John Jeavons and Carol Cox, *The Sustainable Vegetable Garden*.

## Square Foot Gardening

There is one more bio-intensive method to discuss here, one that was created with geeks in mind. It was invented by an engineer named Mel Bartholomew. Back in the 1980s, he was searching for a better way to garden. He wanted to reduce the space needed to grow food, decrease water, and eliminate as much labor as possible. As engineers often do, he questioned everything. In particular, he questioned traditional row farming. After a successful television series on PBS and a book outlining all the details of his innovative method, millions of gardeners have adopted his way of doing things.

Beets and carrots planted using SFG spacing techniques (without physical grids, which Mel insists on using for true SFG).

*Square Foot Gardening*, as the name implies, is based on using square feet instead of rows to plot out crops. Based on a 4' × 4' raised bed, Bartholomew claimed you could grow a laundry list of vegetables in one bed, including one head each of broccoli, cauliflower, and cabbage; sixteen heads of lettuce; five pounds of peas; sixteen scallions; thirty-two carrots; thirty-two beets (with greens); thirty-two radishes; eight Swiss chard plants; nine spinach plants; and nine turnips. Sound impossible? Not so.

His method divides square feet equally into sections, like a four-square or tic-tac-toe board, depending on how far apart plants need to be spaced. If plants need to be 12" apart, plant one in the center of each square foot and *poof!* Those plants are 12" apart. Vegetables like lettuces generally need to be 6" apart. By dividing a square foot into four quarters, and planting one lettuce in the center of each quarter, those lettuces are all 6" apart from each other. That's four lettuces per square foot. If you only have a balcony, using this method you can grow enough salad greens in 2 square feet to make salads for one person for three months. Just harvest the outside leaves and those eight heads of lettuce will keep producing all season long.

Much like other bio-intensive methods, Bartholomew's technique of planting vegetables close together creates that living mulch we were talking about earlier. Plant shoulders touch, blocking out the sun and keeping soil moist and weed free. That equals less labor and water, and more food for gardeners.

The strategy behind using raised beds no larger than 4' × 4' is simple. An adult can reach about 2' into a garden without stepping on the soil. If you have access on all four sides, you will be able to access the entire raised bed easily. If you situate your bed up against the wall, the bed should be narrower to accommodate only having access on three sides, even less if access is only available on one side.

By dividing the 4' × 4' raised bed into 16 square feet, Bartholomew discovered that each square could be worked individually. For example, let's say we have radishes planted in one square and lettuces in a second square next to it. Radishes sprout and grow quickly, and will be ready to harvest long before the lettuces. According to Bartholomew, you can harvest those radishes, and then use a hand trowel to add a handful of compost to that now-empty square. Then it's ready to plant again without ever disturbing the lettuces next door. In fact, after initial setup, you can work your garden without ever using a shovel again.

*Square Foot Gardening* has its own soil formula, method of starting seeds, and plenty of shortcuts to reduce waste, including seeds. Traditional farming (and instructions on every seed packet) will have you sprinkling seeds in a row, backfilling the soil to cover the seeds, watering the entire row, and waiting for the seeds to sprout. Once they do, you have to go back and thin—pull or cut out any sprout that is not a certain distance from its neighbor. What a waste of seeds, time, and energy. Bartholomew's method has you drilling holes exactly where the seeds are going to grow to maturity. You drop in a seed or two, cover it up, and water 1 square foot instead of a long row. A germination test will help determine seed viability, so you don't waste time planting seeds that won't germinate.

In his original book, Bartholomew developed a geeky way to plant seeds. It goes like this: drill a hole that is twice as deep as the recommended seed depth. Fill the hole halfway with vermiculite.

## GEEKY GARDENING TIP

### GERMINATION TEST

Do you know where your seeds have been? Out baking in the sun, taking a dip in the fountain? A germination test is one sure way to know whether your seeds are past their prime or not. Lay a paper towel on a flat surface and put ten seeds in a straight line across the center, about ½" or so apart. Fold the paper towel up around the seeds, keeping it flat. Run the towel under a stream of water to dampen it. Place the whole thing in a plastic bag. Seal the bag and place it on top of your refrigerator out of direct light. Check back to make sure the towel stays wet. Seed packets will state "Days to Germination," so mark your calendar and check for sprouts when time is up. If seven out of ten seeds germinate, you're in pretty good shape. If five out of ten seeds germinate, that's a 50 percent germination ratio, so double up on the number of seeds you plant in each hole. If less than 50 percent sprout, plant the remainder of the packet in a fit of passion or swap them for newer seeds.

Drop in a seed. Fill the rest of the hole with more vermiculite. Vermiculite, as mentioned earlier, holds moisture exceedingly well. By creating a moisture cocoon around your seeds, you're ensuring they won't dry out. The other thing that makes this technique cool is you now know exactly where your seeds are planted (vermiculite is cream-colored and shiny), and you know exactly where to water. Not only that—you will know exactly where to replant if your seeds don't emerge.

The great thing about *Square Foot Gardening* is that it's malleable. You can adapt it to any size or space. Make "L" shapes in corners, long narrow planters alongside yards, or create a child's garden with smaller raised beds. *Square Foot Gardening* advises ways to modify raised beds for concrete patios, or elevate them for those in wheelchairs. It also maintains you can save space by growing up instead of out.

Vertical gardening has become more popular in recent years, but Bartholomew has been preaching the benefits of growing crops up trellises long before it was hip to plant a living roof or wall. Sure, we're accustomed to seeing crops like cucumbers and pole beans winding up a trellis, but what about cantaloupe or butternut squash? It's totally possible with SFG. Here's a chance to use that ratty old T-shirt or those pantyhose with an unsightly run. As fruit develops, you can fashion a sling from the sleeves of dad's old sweatshirt and tie it securely to the trellis. Melons ripen without pulling down the vines because they are fully supported.

While each of these bio-intensive methods can be used individually, adventurous gardeners can combine the techniques to see just how efficient their garden can be. Try hexagonal spacing and vertical gardening together. Play with double digging and formal raised beds to see if you can improve yields. These techniques came about from years of trial and error, and finally success. You may come up with the next best bio-intensive method yet.

## Manipulating Sunlight

Small-space gardeners are often faced with more than just space constraints. Apartment and condo dwellers also have to deal with sun exposure, or the lack thereof. With people stacked on top of one another in urban communities, it can be difficult to find a spot that has full sun—at least six hours of sunlight each day. One solution is to head to the roof, but if that's not an option, what else can you do?

### Get Some Wheels

Plant in containers that are outfitted with casters so you can roll the pots to the sunny parts of the balcony, patio, or yard as needed. This way you can gain several hours of sunlight.

### Elevate

Sometimes a little height can do wonders. Here's an example: A woman had a corner garden plot that would get decent sun were it not in the shadow of an annoying staircase that blocked light from ever touching the soil. She found an old cane chair with a broken seat and relocated a pot to fit snugly in the seat of the chair. By elevating her containers just a couple feet, they were now tall enough to reach sunlight. The plants thrived and climbed up the staircase railing to the second floor.

### Reflect

White boards are widely used in the film and television industry to bounce light into a dark corner. They work for gardens, too. A word of warning, though: just stick to white boards, rather than mirrors or other focused light reflectors. The point is not to fry your plants, just to extend their exposure to light.

### Add a Grow Light

If you are gardening up against a wall with access to electricity, you can install a powerful grow light (like the kind used in greenhouses or hydroponics) with full-spectrum light bulbs to extend daylight exposure. Some high-powered lights require a ballast to prevent flickering or power surges. Generally speaking, grow lights work best when they are within 3" of plant surfaces, so this may not be an option for gardens of varying sizes.

### No Space?

There are other options to try if your garden space isn't much of a garden space. Yard sharing organizations such as Hyperlocavore (*www.hyperlocavore.ning.com*) and UrbanGardenShare (*www.urbangardenshare.org*) match up people who want to garden with people who have yards they don't want to tend. Join a community garden (or get on the waiting list for one) and enjoy your own plot of land for a yearly fee. Don't know of any gardens near you? You can search for one on the American Community Garden Association's website (*www.communitygarden.org*). Just plug in your zip code and see what secret gardens await you.

## ECOLOGY ACTION: A FIELD TRIP TO A GROW BIOINTENSIVE FARM

A foggy November morning in Willits, California, marks the first day of a GROW BIOINTENSIVE workshop, complete with a visit to the Ecology Action Test Farm. The tour includes a walk through the gardens, along the compost heap area, past the seeding tables, and a quick nod to the legal "humanure" composting toilet on site. Several interns show the way, explaining how their well-placed cold frames extend the harvest. They demonstrate how to build a GROW BIOINTENSIVE compost pile with measured buckets of mature and immature biomass. They illustrate the meticulous process of seed germination that begins with pressing seeds into flats of soil, and ends with planting delicate seedlings out in the garden. They show off their compost crops in action—permanent alfalfa beds that have been producing nitrogen-rich green biomass for fifteen years. Down the path near the center of the Circle Garden, interns point out a stand of 6'-tall tree collards of descending height in a nearby mounded raised bed. The collards are on a four-year rotation, with new collards planted each year, and the oldest pulled out after year four. These tree collards demonstrate how choosing perennial plants over annuals increases overall yield. Bigger plants produce more, and the soil doesn't have to be conditioned each year. It saves time, energy, and water—because older plants have deep root systems.

Despite the fact that the farm looks healthy and prolific, John Jeavons, in his ever-present tweed coat and golfer's cap, says the land is high in nickel, so they have

Ecology Action Test Farm's Garden Circle.

Cold frames and cover crops in 100-square-foot beds on the hillside.

trouble getting high yields at Ecology Action compared to their other test garden a few miles away.

Perhaps the most charming part of the garden is what they call the Medicine Cabinet—the medicinal herb garden near the Circle. Feverfew, chamomile, and self heal are labeled with hand-painted plant markers.

It is tempting to pick a leaf here and there to sample the tasty greens on the property, but the interns ask guests to refrain from doing so, since they are required to weigh and measure every single piece of fruit, every pound of grain, and every gram of biomass that is generated from the garden. One of the interns, who is leaving at the end of the year, said with a smile that she looks forward to eating food right in the garden without weighing it first.

Visiting the Ecology Action Test Farm gives students who have traveled from all around the world a chance to see what can be accomplished on less than a quarter acre of land. One can't help but leave with a renewed sense of passion for bio-intensive methods and a drive to employ these sustainable techniques at home.

Seeds
Seeds
Seeds

# CHAPTER 6

# PLANTING NITTY-GRITTY

Okay, you've done your bed prep, you've planned out your growing space, you've chosen what to grow based on your hardiness zone and frost dates. Now it's time to get down to the nitty-gritty and plant something. In this chapter, you will learn what to do with all those seeds and transplants from the nursery. We'll cover step-by-step instructions for planting as well as how to grow specific vegetables each season. You'll learn about the difference between heirloom and open-pollinated seeds, hybrids, and GMOs. You'll even find out how to choose a good plant from the nursery if you decide not to grow from seed. Before you get soiled, though (sorry, couldn't resist a pun like that), let's talk about how to store your seeds so they remain viable year after year.

## Seed Storage the Garden Geek Way

Seeds are wonderful things. They contain all the genetic information they need to germinate and grow into a food-producing plant. With a little help from you, adding soil and nutrients to the mix, seeds will thrive and reward your efforts with fresh fruit, abundant greens, and delicious vegetables for several months. It all starts with viable seed. In Chapter 5 we talked about doing a germination test, but here are the tricks for storing seeds so your germination rates are higher. You may have heard you should replace your seeds every year or so. If you play your cards right and store them properly, you won't need to buy new seeds. You'll be able to use those same seeds for years to come.

### Storing Seeds

Seeds need three things in order to grow: light, heat (or at least warmth), and moisture. The three factors that ensure successful germination are the same factors that will cause seeds to lose viability during storage. By keeping your seeds in the sun, storing them in a hot attic, or laying the packets down on wet soil, you will send your seeds to an early grave. Conversely, if you keep your seeds cool, dark, and dry, they will perform year after year with relative consistency.

So where is a cool, dark, and dry place in your home? Maybe it's a closet, or a well-insulated garage. Believe it or not, your refrigerator is the best place to store seeds. But let's not just throw packets in there willy-nilly. There's a method to all of this. Start with a jar that has a lid. Ideally it should be a jar you can fit your hand inside. If nothing in your house fits that description, try a plastic or glass container with a tight-fitting lid.

**GEEKY GARDENING TIP**

**EASY SEEDS TO SAVE**

Some seeds require no skill whatsoever in order to save them. Try growing and saving these seeds for starters:

- Beans
- Lettuce
- Peas
- Sweet peppers
- Tomatoes

Now scavenge your closet and pantry for a few desiccant packets. You know—those white pouches that come inside packaging when you buy vitamins, shoes, or stereo equipment. They keep moisture away and are perfect for your new seed jar. Toss them in the bottom, and then insert your seed packets. Close the lid and store the jar in the fridge. That's it.

## How to Plant from Seed

When you're ready to plant, remove your seeds from the fridge, grab your garden plan, and head for the great outdoors. If you know exactly what you're going to plant, you might want to take those seeds out of the jar and keep them in your pocket. If the whole jar is making the trip to the garden, then be sure to set it down in a shady place out of direct sunlight.

There are several ways to plant seeds. Most seed packets will offer plenty of advice about how deep to plant and how far apart. If you've misplaced your seed packet, see the Geeky Gardening Tip about Seed Depth for help.

If you are using a bio-intensive method of planting, measure the distance between your plants based on the "space after thinning" dimension on the seed packet and mark the soil. If you are drilling holes with your finger, here's a useful trick: wet your planting area first. Dry soil will not hold a shape when you drill a planting hole, it will just collapse in on itself. Save time by watering the soil just a bit. You don't want to soak it, just give it enough moisture to hold together without collapsing.

If you want to plant in rows, use the edge of your hand or a hand trowel to cut a shallow trench into the soil. Some gardeners prefer to use a hoe for the task. It's all good. Just remember seeds aren't planted very deep. If you get too enthusiastic, your ½"-deep trench will be 2½" deep. For those who tend toward OCD, you can lay a rake handle down and press it into the soil for a perfect line. Lift the rake, distribute your seeds, and backfill the soil into place.

To prevent dumping all your seeds out onto the soil at once, take your

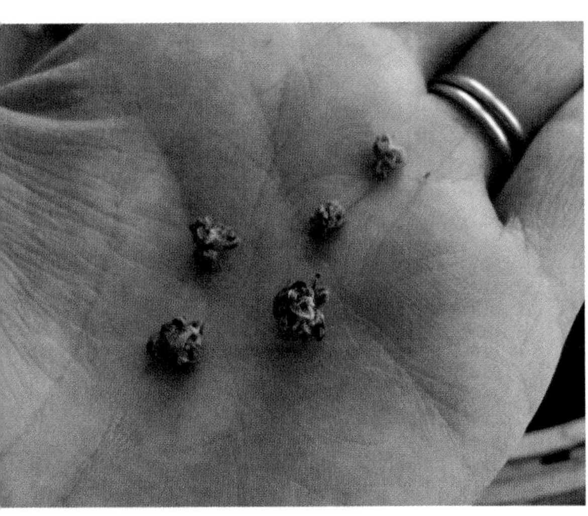

Chard seeds are really clusters of seeds. More than one seed germinates from each cluster.

gloves off and pour a small number of seeds into your nondominant hand. Use the thumb and index finger of your dominant hand to swizzle a seed or two into each planting hole or along a trench. Return the unused seeds to the packet by holding the seed packet by the outer edges and squeezing the packet so it opens up like a mouth. Cup the hand with the seeds and tip the seeds back into the packet. It's not rocket science, but you'd be surprised how many people have trouble getting those little buggers back to safety.

> **GEEKY GARDENING TIP**
>
> **SEED DEPTH**
>
> The general rule of thumb is to plant a seed twice as deep as the width of the seed—and that's across the belly, not head to toe. For example, lettuce seeds are very small, and if you put two of them side by side, the distance would be about ⅛" across. It's no coincidence that the typical planting depth recommended for lettuce seeds happens to be ⅛". Another example: side-by-side, two squash seeds range between ½"–1" wide, so you would plant those between ½"–1" deep. It's a neat trick to remember when you lose the seed packet, or you trade seeds with someone without copying the information down. Some experts will tell you to plant three times the depth of the seed; feel free to try that, but remember that seeds planted too deep may rot instead of sprouting.

## How to Plant from Nursery Stock

Transplants, or starts, from nurseries can save time and prevent failures for new gardeners. Local garden centers sell tried-and-true varieties that are nearly guaranteed to grow in your hardiness zone. You can pick up a 4" pot or six-pack of lettuces on the weekend and be harvesting outer leaves a month later. Essentially, nursery stock saves you about six weeks over growing from seed. The downside of buying nursery stock is you are limited to what they have on hand. That said, the array of available heirlooms and more unusual varieties is broadening each year as gardeners demand them.

While most nurseries keep their selection fresh, some less-reputable garden centers continue to sell transplants that are past their prime. Unsuspecting new gardeners wouldn't know any better, so here are some tips to know how to pick a good plant from the nursery.

### Choose Small, Stout Plants

Remember that a plant has foliage above and roots below. Plant roots go down (or would if they had room) as far as the foliage reaches upward. So if you see a plant

in a 4" pot with a foot or two of foliage above the soil level, pass on it. Opt for stocky plants that are just getting their start. The balance of roots to foliage is more equal and those plants will thrive when transplanted. Sometimes you will find a plant that has a spindly stem with lots of distance between leaf sets. That's a leggy plant. Leggy plants didn't get enough sun, and are not good candidates for your garden. Resist the urge to rescue the underdog—choose the stocky plant instead.

### Watch Out for Diseases

A few yellow leaves here and there isn't a bad thing, but if you see signs of powdery mildew or blight on a plant, don't take it home. Withered leaves, brown splotches, and fuzzy white patches on leaves are a sure sign of disease. Since the whole point of starting with transplants is to increase your success rate and shorten your growing time, start with healthy plants.

### Avoid Flowers or Fruit

It's so tempting to buy a vegetable start that is already flowering or setting fruit. The hard work is already done for you, right? Not quite. Once a plant starts to produce fruit, the focus is no longer on root development. When you buy a transplant, you want the plant to focus on root development first, flowering and fruiting later. If you do find yourself having to choose from veggie plants with flowers or fruit, pinch those off to refocus the plant's energy on root production. You'll end up with a higher-yielding plant in the long run.

Once you've chosen your nursery stock, it's important to plant them properly. Sure, you could just pull them out of the pot and plop them in the soil, but you'll give your plants a fighting chance if you take an extra step or two.

First, water the transplants well. Some gardeners like to submerge the pots in a bucket of water just above the soil level until air bubbles stop rising up. A good drenching will accomplish the same thing. Next, dig your planting hole just as deep as your pot. You can set the transplant into the planting hole while it's still in the pot to see if the soil levels align. Not deep enough? Lift out the plant and keep digging. Some plants, such as tomatoes, can be buried deeper than the existing soil level, but most plants prefer to be put in at the same level. Throw a handful of fertilizer in the hole and scratch it in with your fingers. Mix it in well to avoid direct contact with plant roots. If you have amended your beds before planting, this step is not necessary. Squeeze the pot around the sides to loosen the soil and more easily remove the root ball.

Place your thumb and forefinger (or do the Spock "Live long and prosper" thing if you want) on either side of the plant stem, then flip the plant upside down so the root ball is facing up and the foliage faces down. Pull off the pot.

Now comes the part many gardeners leave out. Take the bottom of the root ball in your hands and tease the roots apart with your fingers. Just pull the soil and roots apart a little bit to open them up and give them guidance—you're pointing them in a new direction. Some gardeners use scissors to trim the roots to trigger a new growth process. It isn't necessary, but if you feel compelled, go ahead and give it a try. Now your plant is ready to go in the ground.

Set the plant upright in the planting hole and gently backfill the soil around it. Be careful not to compact the soil. Instead, leave it loose, and let water do the job for you. By watering the soil immediately afterward, it naturally removes air pockets and settles the soil around your plants. You may need to add more soil to fill in sunken spots, but that's better than to have squeezed all the air out of your soil.

To help plants recover from possible transplant shock, which can make them wilt or suffer a setback within a week or two after planting, water newly transplanted crops with a mixture of water and kelp emulsion. As mentioned earlier, kelp emulsion or liquid kelp extract contains a broad spectrum of minerals and naturally occurring growth hormones that help ease plants into their new home.

Now that you have the basics of how to plant from seed and from nursery stock, it's a good time to talk about specific plants. The next section profiles an array of easy-to-grow vegetables that are suitable for small space gardeners and beginners as well as veteran green thumbs. As you grow your garden, use these plant profiles to help guide your way through the season. Note: Plant spacing is based on bio-intensive methods. Those using row farming techniques would space these farther apart than what is suggested here.

# ALL ABOUT SEEDS: HEIRLOOM, OPEN-POLLINATED, AND HYBRID SEEDS

When you're ready to dive into planting your garden from seeds rather than transplants, there are a few things to know about seeds before you amass your collection. Seeds embody history. They contain stories from past generations and tell us about the climates and conditions they have adapted to over the centuries. There are seeds that have naturally cross-pollinated over generations to become stronger and well adapted to certain climates. Then there are new seeds, developed by careful hybridization, that feature desirable traits like deeper colors, larger fruit, or stronger disease resistance. Let's talk about these individually.

- **Heirloom**—Anything that has been handed down from generation to generation is considered an heirloom. While some antique dealers say an heirloom has to be at least 100 years old, there is no specific time frame associated with heirloom seeds. The general consensus, however, is that seeds found in existence prior to the 1950s can be called heirlooms. Why the 1950s? Because that's when the first hybrid seeds were put into commercial production (even though some sources say hybrids were used as far back as the 1930s). An heirloom is an open-pollinated seed (we'll talk about that next) that was not used in commercial agriculture. Heirloom varieties are often regional or rare. Once you start growing heirlooms, you'll never be satisfied with boring old market-variety produce again.
- **Open-Pollinated**—These plants are the result of cross-pollinating via the wind, birds, or bees. Seeds saved from these plants will produce plants just like their parents. In other words, they breed "true to type." If you plant the

seeds that were saved from an open-pollinated plant, the resulting plant will look and taste just like its parent. Theoretically, as you save seeds year after year from plants that thrived in your garden, those seeds will produce stronger, well-adapted plants for your climate. Just keep this part straight: an heirloom is open-pollinated, but not all open-pollinated seeds are heirlooms. Both types of seeds are exactly what you want to have on hand for survival when the zombie apocalypse strikes.

- **Hybrid—**A hybrid seed is produced with human intervention, by crossing two different parent plants, usually from the same species. Because this generally occurs in a controlled environment, nature can't reproduce it, so the process has to be duplicated each year by breeders in order to get the same results. In other words, seeds saved from hybridized plants don't breed true to type. They will revert back to some other part of their genetics and are therefore not reliable for seed saving.
- **GMOs—**Let's not confuse hybrids with genetically modified organisms (GMOs). Hybridization occurs under controlled conditions, but genetic modification occurs under a microscope. Strands of DNA are cut and spliced, replacing part of the vegetable's natural genetic makeup with something from another organism. Like an organ transplant process, the organism can reject the transplant (in this case, foreign DNA), so biotechnologists use what's called a viral promoter to ensure the new DNA takes. Virtually every GMO out there was created by inserting Cauliflower Mosaic Virus into the DNA strands. There's a plethora of disconcerting information about this fact, and if you want to read more, start with the Institute for Responsible Technology (*www.responsibletechnology.org*).

  Examples of GMO technology: some tomatoes have been genetically modified to contain higher levels of nutrients by splicing fish genes into tomato DNA. GMO corn has been altered to produce its own pesticides. Soybean crops have been modified to withstand constant applications of systemic weed killers. While the debate goes on about whether GMO foods are safe to consume, the organic industry is steering clear of them. So at this time, if you buy organic seeds or produce, they are GMO free (barring the ever-increasing cross-contamination from wind-pollinated GMO crops.) Currently GMO seeds are not available to home gardeners. Look for seed catalogs from companies that subscribe to the Safe Seed Pledge, which states that the company does not knowingly or willingly grow or sell GMO seeds. Flip to Appendix B to find a list of Trusted Seed Companies as well as Great Geeky Heirloom/Open-Pollinated Seeds to Try.

# Vegetables

## Arugula

Latin Name: *Eruca sativa*

Seed Planting Depth: ¼– ½"

Plant Spacing: 4–6"

Soil Temp. for Germ.: 45°–70°F

Sun: Full to partial

Water: Moderate

Days to Germinate: 3–7

Days to Maturity: 25–45

### About Arugula

Arugula is an annual plant native to the Mediterranean and has been grown since Roman times, both in the wild and in commercial agriculture. Its leaves are peppery and look similar to radish leaves. The leaves, blossoms, seedpods, and mature seeds of the plant are all edible. Though typically used raw in salads to add a spicy punch to other greens, it can also be cooked with pasta or meats or pureed into a sauce. In traditional southern European dishes, the leaves are also used on pizzas and in pesto.

### Growing Arugula

Arugula seed is best sown directly into the garden where you intend to grow it to maturity. Plant the seeds 4–6" apart. Gently cover them with ¼" of soil and water. Arugula prefers a cool soil temperature and tends to bolt to seed in summer heat, so grow it in the fall/winter and spring seasons. Plant in fertile, loose soil. Water every day until the seeds germinate. Then, water them as needed to keep the soil moist but not soggy.

### Harvesting Arugula

The seeds should sprout in three to seven days (slightly longer in cooler temperatures). For a continuous crop, sow more seeds every two weeks to ensure new cuttings are available at regular intervals. Arugula matures very quickly—typically within forty days—so get ready to start harvesting in as little as four weeks. Harvest the outside leaves while they are young and tender. The larger arugula gets, the more pungent it becomes. Allow the hardiest plants to bolt to seed and set flowers. When the pods become dry and brittle, carefully remove them from the plant and crush them over a bowl. Six to eight seeds will be found in each pod. Place them in a labeled envelope or plastic bag to keep for future use. At the end of the season, pull and compost any remaining plants and roots.

## Beans

Latin Name: *Phaseolus vulgaris*
Planting Depth: ¾–1½"
Plant Spacing: 4–6"
Soil Temp. for Germ.: 70°–85°F
Sun: Full
Water: Moderate
Days to Germinate: 6–12
Days to Maturity: 55–60

### About Beans

Beans are available as bush or pole varieties and yield well, requiring very little work. If you have limited trellis space, opt for bush beans, since they don't require trellising. Pole beans need support, but provide multiple harvests if allowed to grow as a perennial.

### Growing Beans

Beans should be planted after threat of frost is passed. Plant seeds about 1" deep, about 4" apart for bush varieties, and 6" apart for pole beans. Soak bean seeds overnight before planting (but no longer than eight hours or they might rot) and coat them with a bean inoculant to increase germination success. Keep the seed bed moist until germination occurs. Water them regularly thereafter. For a continuous supply of snap beans through spring and summer, plant more seeds every two to four weeks until early August.

### Harvesting Beans

Beans can be harvested fresh or left to dry on the vine for soup/dry beans. For fresh beans, choose pods that are firm, but pick them before the seeds within the pods have filled out—they will be more tender. Wait until morning dew is dried before picking to prevent the spread of bean bacterial blight. Hold the stem with one hand, and pull the pods with the other. This prevents breaking tender shoots. Plants will form new flowers and pods if you harvest regularly before the seeds mature.

### Common Problems

Bean mosaic diseases appear as distorted, yellowish green mottled leaves, and inhibit the production of pods. If you notice this in your garden, switch to a mosaic-resistant bean variety. Bacterial bean blight is another culprit. Bright yellow or brown spots on the leaves or water-soaked spots on the pods indicate the presence of the disease. It is a seed-borne disease, so start with disease-free seed, and don't touch the plant while it's wet (it can spread the disease that way). Don't compost the waste unless your compost pile gets hotter than 160°F.

## Beets

Latin Name: *Beta vulgari*
Planting Depth: ½–1"
Plant Spacing: 3"
Soil Temp. for Germ.: 55°–75°F
Sun: Full to partial
Water: Moderate
Days to Germinate: 5–10
Days to Maturity: 55–70

### About Beets

Beets are sweet, nutritious, and easy to grow in just about any conditions. They are available to grow in different varieties, offering a rainbow of colors and shapes: red, purple, gold, or white; round, oval, or cylindrical. If your weather is severe, look for cultivars that tolerate extreme temperatures. To stock your root cellar, look for beets with good keeping qualities.

## Growing Beets

Beets are best sown directly into the soil where you intend to grow them to maturity. Plant beets in early spring (or fall in warm-winter climates). Plant seeds 3" apart, and ½–1" deep. For an ongoing harvest of tender roots, plant seeds every twenty to thirty days from early spring through midsummer. Plan to plant your last beet about four to seven weeks before the first expected frost date.

Beets perform best in full sun but tolerate partial shade, too. They love water, so keep the soil moist. They can withstand freezing temperatures, but young plants exposed to two to three weeks of temperatures below 50°F may go to seed prematurely. Most beet seeds produce a cluster of seedling plants, so you'll want to thin these with scissors when they emerge.

## Harvesting Beets

Beets can be harvested between fifty to seventy days after sowing seeds. For baby beets, harvest sooner. Beet greens are ready to harvest in just thirty to forty-five days. Pull up roots when they are 1½–3" wide. You can check the size by running a finger around the shoulder of the root. Lift them out of the soil carefully to avoid bruising them. Remove any dirt, then cut the tops off, leaving at least 1" of the stem to prevent the roots from bleeding. They can be refrigerated for several weeks, or layered in a box filled with sand or peat and stored in a cool spot for two to five months. Beets can be frozen, canned, or pickled.

## Broccoli

Latin Name: *Brassica oleracea*
Planting Depth: ¼– ½"
Plant Spacing: 12"
Soil Temp. for Germ.: 55°–85°F
Sun: Full
Water: Moderate
Days to Germinate: 5–14
Days to Maturity: 60–90

### About Broccoli

Broccoli is a hardy Cole crop that is high in vitamins A and D and is best grown during the cooler seasons of the year. Broccoli evolved from a wild cabbage plant in Europe as early as the sixth century B.C.E. Since the Roman Empire, broccoli has been considered a uniquely valuable food among Italians. However, it was not until the 1920s that broccoli became a regular dinner feature in the United States.

### Growing Broccoli

Broccoli plants of most varieties can produce a harvest over an entire season if grown properly. Once the center head is harvested, side shoots continue to produce, extending the harvest over several months. In most parts of the country, it is possible to grow two crops per year. For beginning gardeners, transplants are recommended rather than starting from seed, because broccoli can take a while to develop. However, fall crops are okay to direct seed in your garden. Plant one seed or transplant per square foot—or plant a few seeds and then thin. Broccoli plants grow upright with large leaves up to 2½' tall. For spring planting, start seedlings in mid-winter for transplanting into the garden. Be sure all threat of frost has passed before planting in the garden. Water well and fertilize the plants mid-season to encourage heads to form.

### Harvesting Broccoli

Broccoli heads and stems are edible. A large central head will form first, and after that is harvested, smaller side shoots will appear. Cut the central head with 5–6" of stem, when the head is tight with buds and fully developed. If you wait too long, the buds start to loosen and separate and the individual bright yellow flowers start to open. You can still eat it at this point, but it's just not as pretty. Continue harvesting broccoli side shoots, a.k.a. broccolini, for several weeks afterward.

### Common Problems

Cabbage worms and aphids are the biggest problem with most brassicas, but harlequin bugs (*Murgantia histronica*) and bagrada bugs (*Bagrada hilaris*) can be a problem too. Check your brassicas for insects daily—scan the underside of leaves and remove the insects. Keep an eye out for maggots on the stem and roots. Clubroot disease is common in cauliflower, cabbage, broccoli, etc., if crops are not regularly rotated. Roots swell or form "clubs" and interfere with the plant's ability to take up food from the soil. Regular crop rotation will help prevent this disease.

## Carrots

Latin Name: *Daucus carota* var. *sativus*
Planting Depth: ⅛–⅜"
Plant Spacing: 3"
Soil Temp. for Germ.: 50°–80°F
Sun: Full to partial
Water: Moderate
Days to Germinate: 6–18
Days to Maturity: 65–75

### About Carrots

Carrots are an excellent source of beta carotene, which your body converts into vitamin A, a crucial nutrient in maintaining great eyesight. They can be eaten raw or cooked, and are available in color varieties ranging from yellow or white to orange or purple.

### Growing Carrots

Carrots can be grown sixteen per square foot, or hexagonally planted on 3" centers. Seeds can take between fourteen to twenty-one days to sprout, so watch over them carefully and don't forget to water daily. Carrots prefer cool temperatures, so plant in early spring or late fall. High temperatures over 75°F can cause low-quality carrots. Once roots have developed, water the plants as required to keep the soil moist to about 3" deep. Plant in well-amended soil and fertilize as plants grow to ensure proper development (monthly for sandy soil, less often for clay).

### Harvesting Carrots

Depending on the variety, carrots should be ready for harvest approximately fifty-five to seventy-five days after planting. Check the diameter by running a finger around the shoulders of each root to determine size. This will also loosen the soil, making it easier to harvest. When the top of each root is about 1" in diameter, it's ready to pick. To prolong the shelf life of carrots, break off the green tops and compost or juice them—or feed them to your worms or chickens for a tasty treat.

## Cauliflower

Latin Name: *Brassica oleracea*
Planting Depth: ¼–½"
Plant Spacing: 1 per square foot, or 15–18" apart if desired
Soil Temp. for Germ.: 55°–85°F
Sun: Full
Water: Moderate
Days to Germinate: 3–10
Days to Maturity: 70–80

### About Cauliflower

Cauliflower is a cool season vegetable that is considered a delicacy in both India and Malaysia. It is a more advanced crop to grow; gardeners in higher altitude areas tend to have better luck, but don't let that deter you from trying. In warm-winter climates, cauliflower grows best in fall, but no matter where you live, this veggie requires nutrient-rich soil to form a head.

### Growing Cauliflower

Start cauliflower seeds indoors first, then transplant to your garden after six to eight weeks. (One plant per square foot—they get big!) Transplant them to the garden about ten days after the last frost. Water them well with compost tea to prevent wilting, and water regularly to ensure uninterrupted growth.

### Harvesting Cauliflower

Cauliflower is known for its snowy white heads, but it can turn yellow if exposed to direct sunlight. To prevent this, use twine or string to tie the leaves closed like an unopened bud over the heads when the heads are still small like a fist. Check regularly to see if they are ready to harvest. If left too long, cauliflower heads loosen and the tight curds separate, and become less appetizing. Cauliflower is usually ready to harvest about a week after it's been tied up.

### Common Cauliflower Problems

See Broccoli.

## Chard

Latin Name: *Beta vulgaris*
Planting Depth: ½–¾"
Plant Spacing: 6–8"
Soil Temp. for Germ.: 45°–80°F
Sun: Full to partial
Water: Moderate
Days to Germinate: 6–10
Days to Maturity: 55–60

### About Swiss Chard

Swiss chard is a member of the beet family but is grown for its leaves rather than roots. You can find varieties of chard that produce white, yellow, pink, orange, or red stalks. It's great for new gardeners to grow because in some cases plants can last over a year. It is one of the few vegetables that can be grown in partial sun.

### Growing Swiss Chard

Swiss chard can be directly seeded into the garden in early to mid-spring or in fall in warmer climates. The seeds are actually clusters of seeds, so you will get more than one sprout from each seed planted. Thin seedlings to 6–8" apart. Keep the seed bed moist to ensure continuous growth.

### Harvesting Swiss Chard

Start harvesting the outer leaves when there are several sets of leaves and the plant is at least 1' tall. Use a knife, or tear stems off at the base of the plant, but be careful not to pull too hard—twist instead and the stems should tear easily from the plant. Hold the plant with one hand if it is still young while harvesting, otherwise you risk uprooting the whole plant.

Store unwashed leaves in plastic bags with a dry paper towel in the crisper for two to three days. Some gardeners wash the leaves and store them between layers of paper towels in a plastic bag in the fridge. The stalks, which taste like beets, can be stored longer if removed from the leaves. Don't like beets? Cut the stems out and eat just the leaves.

## Collards

Latin Name: *Brassica aleracea*
Planting Depth: ¼"
Plant Spacing: 12"
Soil Temp. for Germ.: 50°–75°F
Sun: Full
Water: Moderate
Days to Germinate: 3–10
Days to Maturity: 65–80

### About Collards

Collards are a cool-season leafy green rich in vitamins and minerals. They tolerate warm weather better than any other member of the cabbage family. Although collard greens are popular in the South, they can also be grown in northern areas because of their ability to withstand frost.

### Growing Collards

Plant seeds in early spring, or in fall in warm-winter climates. If you choose to scatter seeds and then thin, don't toss those thinnings. Throw them into a salad or sauté them instead. Keep the soil moist during hot periods in the summer and control insects and diseases. Collards will reward you with an abundant harvest. Fertilize mid-season to keep plants going strong.

### Harvesting Collards

The leaves and stems are edible and can be harvested at any time once the plant is big enough. Pick the larger outer leaves when the plants are 10–12" tall. Like kale and Swiss chard, collards grow from the center, so leave a few sets of leaves to stimulate future growth.

### Common Problems

See Broccoli for information on aphids and cabbage worms. Use a floating row cover to protect plants from infestation.

## Green Onions

Latin Name: *Allium fistulosum*

Planting Depth: ¼"

Plant Spacing: ranges from no thinning to 3"

Soil Temp. for Germ.: 50°–85°F

Sun: Full

Water: Water often

Days to Germinate: 4–13

Days to Maturity: 60–65

### About Green Onions

Green onions, scallions, or bunching onions are a cool-season vegetable that can be grown successfully throughout most of temperate North America. In warmer climates, green onions can be grown year-round, and while they are technically perennials, they are generally grown as annuals. According to *High Mowing Seeds*, "True bunching onions or scallions, *Allium fistulosum*, do not form bulbs and remain straight and slender; many common onion varieties may be grown as bunching onions, but will eventually bulb up."

### Growing Green Onions

Direct sow seeds in spring or fall by broadcasting (sprinkling seed) or with specific bio-intensive plant-spacing methods. Seeds can take a while to germinate and grow, and they don't like competition, so keep the area well watered and weeded. As with most vegetables, green onions prefer soils with a lot of organic matter.

### Harvesting Green Onions

Pull green onions any time after the green parts are the thickness of a pencil. If left to grow longer, green onions thicken as the taste intensifies. They may be used for cooking when they are too strong to eat raw. Once plants form flower stalks, they are too tough to eat, so let them develop seeds and save those for next year.

### Common Problems

Root maggots can be a problem in higher latitudes. Rust can also settle on green parts of the plant. Cut off affected leaves and thin plants to allow for better air circulation. Rotate crops to prevent rust next year.

## Kale

Latin Name: *Brassica oleracea*
Planting Depth: ¼–½"
Plant Spacing: 12"
Soil Temp. for Germ.: 55°–85°F
Sun: Full to partial
Water: Moderate
Days to Germinate: 5–14
Days to Maturity: 50–60

### About Kale

Kale is the meat of the veggie kingdom—rich in vitamins C and A, and loaded with potassium, calcium, iron, and fiber. Kale can be eaten raw (use an acid like lemon juice or vinegar to make it more digestible) or cooked. Like other brassicas, kale prefers to grow in the cool season, and can become sweeter in winter if grown with protection from frost.

### Growing Kale

Kale loves full sun, but can handle partial exposure if that is all you have. Add plenty of compost or well-rotted manure. Fertilize the plants mid-season with liquid fertilizer or compost tea.

### Harvesting Kale

Harvest the outside leaves, leaving the center bud to grow new leaves. Kale will produce all season long. Cut or tear leaves from the base of the plant when they are about 10–12" long. Kale is delicious in frittatas or cooked in the same way as Swiss chard (see Chard).

### Common Problems

See Broccoli for information on cabbage worms and aphids. Kale is susceptible to fungal and bacterial diseases like head rot, and powdery and downy mildews. Those in coastal areas and other places where these diseases are common should avoid watering from overhead. Check often and remove affected leaves early.

## Kohlrabi

Latin Name: *Brassica oleracea*
Planting Depth: ¼–½"
Plant Spacing: 4–6"
Soil Temp. for Germ.: 60°–65°F
Sun: Full to partial
Water: Moderate
Days to Germinate: 5–10
Days to Maturity: 60–65

### About Kohlrabi

Kohlrabi is another great brassica that is relatively easy to grow. This European veggie came to America in the 1800s, but despite being around for so long, it is still not a household name. It's an odd-looking vegetable with a bulbous body, and leaves that protrude from the top like Sideshow Bob's hair on *The Simpsons*. Don't let that fool you—it has a delicious flavor like broccoli stems and potato. Kohlrabi leaves are also edible.

### Growing Kohlrabi

Sow seeds indoors in early spring, or fall in warm-winter climates. If you plan to thin your seedlings, use them in stir-fries or salads. You could plant more every few weeks for a continuous supply through summer. Like other Cole crops, kohlrabi tolerates some frost. It also can tolerate partial sun, so plant this crop if you have limited exposure.

### Harvesting Kohlrabi

Kohlrabi is best picked when small, but it is not uncommon for gardeners to think bigger is better and let the vegetables grow into the size of softballs. The bulbous part tends to get tough and woody and slightly bitter, so resist the urge to leave kholrabi in the ground too long. Start harvesting when the stems are about 1" in diameter. Peel the tough skin to reveal the inner goodness of this plant. Sauté it in a little olive oil or butter for a very potato-like experience.

### Common Problems

Like other brassicas, cabbage worms are pesky and tend to love kohlrabi—keep your eyes peeled and remove them if found.

## Leeks

Latin Name: *Allium ampeloprasum*
Planting Depth: ¼"
Plant Spacing: 6"
Soil Temp. for Germ.: 55°–80°F
Sun: Full to partial
Water: Water often
Days to Germinate: 4–7
Days to Maturity: 85–90

### About Leeks

Leeks are alliums, part of the onion family. They look like giant green onions, but the green parts are broad and flat rather than round and hollow. Leeks are best known for their pairing with potatoes in soups and stews, and are a good source of vitamin C. This is another easy crop to grow—perfect for the brown thumbs out there! Leeks are especially good to grow in cooler climates.

### Growing Leeks

Leeks like well-amended soil, so prepare garden beds with aged manure or compost and nitrogen-rich fertilizer. Plant seeds in early spring or fall for best results. They will grow in warmer gardening climates, but temperatures over 80°F will cause them to grow more slowly. Leeks prefer plenty of sunshine. For shorter growing seasons, start with nursery transplants instead of seeds. Mound up the soil around the stem, and add more soil to help keep the stems white. You can use paper towel rolls as sleeves to help keep soil in place. Water them regularly and keep the soil moist but not soggy.

### Harvesting Leeks

Some gardeners like to cut away a portion of the top leaves in midsummer. It focuses the plant's energy on growing roots, rather than leaves. Leeks can take up to five months to grow large stems, but they can be harvested as needed when they're smaller. Harvest leeks by pulling, or loosen the soil around the area first and lift them out with a digging fork. Some leeks will cluster together—you will probably end up harvesting those clusters all at once. Leeks store well in the ground, but pull them immediately if they start to send up a flower stalk. The stalk that runs up the center of the leek is tough and inedible.

## Lettuce

Latin Name: *Lactuca sativa*
Planting Depth: ¼"
Plant Spacing: 6"
Soil Temp. for Germ.: 40°–80°F
Sun: Full to partial
Water: Water often
Days to Germinate: 2–15
Days to Maturity: 60–70

### About Lettuce

Lettuce is a cool-weather vegetable that is easy to grow from seed. There are hundreds of interesting varieties to grow that far surpass iceberg and plain ol' romaine. Lettuces can be planted in early spring, or late summer through fall. In hot weather, lettuce tends to bolt to seed and become bitter tasting. Some varieties handle hot weather better than others, so look for slow-bolt varieties if you plan to grow lettuce in summer.

### Growing Lettuce

Plant seeds in well-amended soil and keep the seed bed moist until roots are established. Lettuce has relatively shallow roots, so it can be planted (or interplanted) with crops with deeper root systems. Beware of overwatering, which can lead to diseases and root rot. You can grow lettuce under shade cloth in hot weather to extend the season.

### Harvesting Lettuce

Harvest the outside leaves of "cos" or romaine-type and leaf lettuces whenever they are large enough to use. The plant will continue to produce leaves from the center. Butterhead varieties form loose heads and are generally picked whole by cutting the stem just above the soil level. You can harvest outside leaves for a time and then harvest the entire head when it begins to fill in.

### Common Problems

Aphids and pincher bugs (*Forficula auricularia*, commonly known as earwigs) will congregate on the undersides of leaves and in the nooks and crannies of center foliage. Wet weather or overhead watering can result in leaf rot. Check for snails regularly and drop them into soapy water.

## Mustard Greens

Latin Name: *Brassica juncea*
Planting Depth: ¼–½"
Plant Spacing: 6"
Soil Temp. for Germ.: 45°–85°F
Sun: Full to partial
Water: Moderate
Days to Germinate: 3–10
Days to Maturity: 40–45

### About Mustard Greens

Mustard greens are as easy to grow as lettuces from seed. This cool-season Cole crop can be grown just about anywhere in the United States during early spring or fall. Mustard greens are high in vitamins A and C and are available in many varieties, including purple-leaf types like Osaka, round waxy types like tatsoi, and jagged-edged varieties such as mizuna.

### Growing Mustard Greens

Mustard can be planted prior to the last frost and all through the cool season. Plant again in mid- to late summer for a fall harvest. Mustard, like arugula, is very quick to sprout, so it's great for growing with kids or those who crave instant gratification. Fertilize mid-season and keep free of weeds. Water regularly to keep the soil from drying out.

### Harvesting Mustard Greens

Harvest the outside leaves when they are young—the bigger they get, the more pungent and spicy these leaves become. Once summer heat comes on, mustard greens typically bolt to seed and become too bitter to eat. If you have chickens, they won't mind the bitter taste, so offload the spent plants to your hens. Once plants bolt to seed, you can harvest the seedpods and eat them (they're really spicy!), or save the seed for next year.

### Common Problems

See Broccoli for problems common to all brassicas.

## Peas

Latin Name: *Pisum sativum*
Planting Depth: 1"
Plant Spacing: 3–4"
Soil Temp. for Germ.: 50°–80°F
Sun: Full
Water: Water often
Days to Germinate: 6–14
Days to Maturity: 60–70

### About Peas

Peas are a cool-season vegetable known for being the "garden snack bar" because they rarely make it back into the house uneaten. There are different categories of peas, namely shelling peas, snap peas, and snow peas. Shelling peas require the pod be removed before eating. Snap peas have been developed over the years to feature less fibrous, edible pods. Snow peas have flat, edible pods that are usually harvested while the peas are small and immature. Snow peas are mainly used in Asian dishes. There is another category of pea called the Southern pea or cowpea (think black-eyed peas)—these are completely different, more like beans actually, and are grown as a warm-weather crop.

### Growing Peas

Peas do best in cool weather and should be planted in early spring or fall. In fact, in warm-winter climates, fall crops tend to do better than spring crops. To ensure germination, coat seeds with an inoculant just before planting. Peas should be trellised (though there are some bush varieties that don't require trellises), and while they have tendrils to grab on to supports, it helps to guide them. Check daily and wind tender vines around trellises. Mulch to keep soil cool and moist, and fertilize with compost mid-season.

### Harvesting Peas

Harvest peas every couple of days to keep plants producing. Sugar snaps are best when the pods start to fatten, but pick them before the seeds fill out. If left too long, peas will become fibrous and starchy. Use these for cooking instead of fresh eating. Harvest by holding the main stem, then break or cut peas from them. Resist the urge to pull—vines break easily.

### Common Problems

Fusarium wilt and root-rot diseases appear as yellowing and wilting of the lower leaves. These diseases work their way up the plant and eventually kill it. Powdery mildew is common in coastal areas. Strive for well-drained soil, or choose disease-resistant varieties to prevent Fusarium wilt.

## Peppers

Latin Name: *Capsicum*
Planting Depth: ¼– ½"
Plant Spacing: 12–18"
Soil Temp. for Germ.: 45°–85°F
Sun: Full to partial
Water: Moderate
Days to Germinate: 3–10
Days to Maturity: 40–45

## About Peppers

Peppers are hot-weather crops that are technically fruits. They aren't as easy to grow as lettuces and tomatoes, but they are worth having in the garden because of the incredible seed varieties available. They require high temperatures, and tend to grow slowly. Sweet bell pepper varieties are grown for stuffing, and a seemingly endless variety of chile peppers (pimiento, cayenne, chile, and paprika) may be grown for food, spices, or as ornamentals. Beginners will benefit by planting nursery stock.

## Growing Peppers

Because of their persnickety nature, pepper seeds should be started indoors in late winter and then transplanted out after nighttime temperatures are above 55°F. Avoid planting them in cold, wet soil. Peppers are heavy feeders, so amend the soil with plenty of organic matter. Water them with compost tea after transplanting. Fertilize after the first flush of peppers set fruit. Keep the plants evenly watered during the harvest season, as inadequate or irregular watering can cause fruit to drop.

## Harvesting Peppers

Peppers can be harvested at any size, depending on the variety. Seed packets will help you determine the right time to harvest specific varieties. Some peppers are picked when green, but many continue to turn red, yellow, or orange as they mature. Ripe peppers generally break away easily from the plant, but proceed carefully or use shears to cut the stems, so as not to damage the rest of the plant. Chile peppers can be used fresh or dried for later use. Be careful when handling chile peppers—capsaicin, the heat component in peppers, can cause eye irritation and burning. Use gloves and wash your hands well after handling.

### Common Problems

Aphids can make a home on weak pepper plants. Maintain healthy soil and nutrient levels and this will not be a problem. Since peppers are in the *Solanaceae* family, they can be susceptible to the same diseases as tomatoes and eggplant. Rotate crops yearly to prevent infection.

## Potatoes

Latin Name: *Solanum tuberosum*
Planting Depth: 2–6"
Plant Spacing: 6–12"
Soil Temp. for Germ.: 60°–70°F
Sun: Full
Water: Moderate
Days to Germinate: 15–21
Days to Maturity: 70–135

### About Potatoes

Potatoes are tubers planted in the cool season. Rather than planted from seed, they are grown from potato cuttings (called seed potatoes). There are at least 100 varieties of potatoes, ranging from soft or waxy and moist, to mealy or firm and dry. There are early, mid-season, and late varieties that work for gardeners in every hardiness zone. You can strategize an extended harvest period (rather than having to harvest all at once) by planting potatoes with both short and long days to maturity. Choose potatoes based on how you like to use them. For example, if you like baked potatoes, choose varieties like Butte, Yukon Gold, or Rose Finn Apple. For sautéed potatoes try Cranberry Red or All Blue.

### Growing Potatoes

There are different schools of thought about growing potatoes. Some farmers plant shallowly (between 1–3" deep) and then add 6" of straw or other mulch over the soil. Others plant deeper (about 6") and forgo mulch. Both work. If you live in the North, plant shallow. If you make your home in the South, plant deeper. Either way, more potatoes develop underground if you "hill up" soil or mulch around the plant as it grows. Some gardeners mound soil around the base; others cover almost all of the foliage with soil, leaving only the top few sets of leaves exposed. The goal is to produce more potatoes and protect surface-dwelling tubers from exposure to sun. Too much sun exposure causes a toxic substance called solanin to develop, which appears as a green hue on the skin. Plant in well-amended soil and use seed potatoes that have developed at least two eyes. It helps to add organic vegetable fertilizer to the bottom of the trench before planting. Potatoes like foliar feeding with kelp and fish emulsion.

### Harvesting Potatoes

"New potatoes" can be harvested when flowers appear. Pick these without uprooting the plant; gently excavate a few from the sides of the plant while it is still growing. Their foliage will begin to turn brown and die back when potatoes are nearing harvest. Cut back water at this point. Stop watering about a week before you plan to harvest, then harvest when all the foliage is dead. Lift the potatoes with a digging fork or dig with your bare hands to expose the tubers. This is great to do with kids. Potato skins are soft and scrape easily, so be careful when harvesting with tools. Use damaged potatoes immediately, but leave the rest on screens or newspaper out of direct sunlight for a week or so to cure before storing.

### Common Problems

Colorado potato beetles, flea beetles, and leafhoppers are the biggest problems with potatoes. Hand picking pests is recommended. Use floating row cover to protect plants from infestation, and practice crop rotation to keep crops disease free.

## Radishes

Latin Name: *Raphanus sativus*
Planting Depth: ½"
Plant Spacing: 3–4"
Soil Temp. for Germ.: 45°–80°F
Sun: Full
Water: Water often
Days to Germinate: 3–6
Days to Maturity: 21–24

### About Radishes

Radishes are some of the easiest vegetables to grow and are perfect for gardeners with short attention spans since they sprout quickly and can be harvested within barely a month of planting. Radishes are best grown during the cool season, but some varieties are bred for warmer weather.

### Growing Radishes

Sow seeds directly in the ground where the plants will mature. Radishes tolerate most soils, as long as the soil is fertilized before planting and has adequate moisture. If radishes are not well watered or fed, they can develop slowly, causing them to become woody and spicy. Run a finger through the soil around the diameter of the radish to determine its size before harvesting.

### Harvesting Radishes

Pick radishes when they are about 1" in diameter. If grown in the fall, they can stay in the ground longer and be picked as needed once they reach mature size. Both greens and roots are edible and can be used raw in salads or roasted for a delicious treat (see Chapter 10).

### Common Problems

In northern latitudes, root maggots can be common. They tunnel into the radishes and leave them in an unsightly state. Garden fabric (floating row cover) will help prevent flies from laying eggs in the soil. Pill and sow bugs (roly-polies) also have been known to nibble away at the tops of radishes. Sprinkle diatomaceous earth to help keep them at bay. Beneficial nematodes can be applied to the soil to help eradicate them as well.

## Spinach

Latin Name: *Spinacea oleracea*
Planting Depth: ½"
Plant Spacing: 4–6"
Soil Temp. for Germ.: 52°–60°F
Sun: Full to partial
Water: Moderate
Days to Germinate: 3–8
Days to Maturity: 40–45

### About Spinach

Spinach is one of the most highly pesticide-laden commercial crops, so it's definitely one to grow at home. You may remember Popeye and his penchant for eating spinach to get stronger. No wonder—it contains vitamin A, iron, calcium, and protein. Spinach can be grown in spring or fall, during cool weather, and is available in savoy (crinkled) or smooth-leaf varieties.

### Growing Spinach

Spinach can be direct seeded or started in flats in early spring or late summer. Plants prefer well-amended soil that drains well. Use floating row cover if you're direct seeding, as birds like to hunt for freshly planted spinach seeds. Plant another batch of seeds every two or three weeks for a continuous supply. Fertilize the plants mid-season as needed (if leaves look yellow or small).

### Harvesting Spinach

Harvest the outside leaves, or cut the whole plant at or just below the soil surface. Spinach is of best quality if it's cut while young. Some gardeners prefer to pick the outer leaves when they are 3" long and allow the younger leaves to develop for later harvest. Once spinach begins to bolt to seed, harvest the entire remaining plant and use it quickly.

### Common Problems

Spinach is susceptible to blight caused by the cucumber mosaic virus. If your climate is humid or wet, opt for resistant varieties to avoid fungal diseases. Various insects love to munch on spinach. Continue using floating row cover as protection, and regularly check the undersides of leaves for snails and other critters. Drop those in soapy water.

## Squash, Summer

Latin Name: *Cucurbita pepo*
Planting Depth: ½–1"
Plant Spacing: 3'
Soil Temp. for Germ.: 65°–90°F
Sun: Full
Water: Moderate
Days to Germinate: 3–8
Days to Maturity: 50–55

### About Summer Squash

Summer squash is a summer staple in the form of zucchini, patty pan, and crookneck squashes. They are planted as the weather warms up in mid-spring and provide all-season harvests. You only need one zucchini plant because it will produce fruit until you're sick of it. Summer squash notoriously grows into baseball bat–sized fruits while gardeners are away on vacation. Pick them regularly to ensure the plant will keep setting fruit.

### Growing Summer Squash

Squash needs space, so allow at least 3' in diameter for each plant. Plant the seeds in a triangle (several seeds in each hole) in the center of the space, and thin to the strongest plants as they develop leaves. Amend the soil in the entire area to allow roots to feed in all directions. Mulch around the plants to retain moisture and keep roots cool. Typically, gardeners will plant squash on hills—raised mounds that allow for drainage—but in sandy soils the opposite works better; plant seeds in a depression so water collects at the roots when irrigating. You can also create a moat around the plant to deliver water to root systems more easily. If fruits turn yellow and drop off, that indicates a lack of pollination. Hand pollinate with a paintbrush by taking pollen from the anthers of the male flowers (which have a long stem) and painting it on the stigma of the female flowers (which have fruit forming beneath them).

### Harvesting Summer Squash

Harvest daily once squash reaches a desired size. They can be picked as small as 3" long, or let grow to club size for stuffing. Generally, summer squash becomes seedy as it grows, so harvest it young for best results. The delicate flowers can be harvested and stuffed, battered, and fried.

### Common Problems

As a member of the cucurbit family, squash can be susceptible to cucumber beetles and vine borers. Squash bugs are other common pests that plague winter and summer squash, cucumbers, and melons. Bugs, nymphs, and eggs can be removed by hand and dropped into soapy water. Remove mulch if pests are sighted early on. Organic sprays are available as a last resort to control populations. Powdery mildew is common in coastal areas. Remove affected leaves or use a mixture of 50 percent water, 50 percent milk to spray on the leaves. Studies show this helps prevent the spread of the fungus.

## Squash, Winter

Latin Name: *Cucurbita maxima, C. pepo, C. moschata*
Planting Depth: 1"
Plant Spacing: 3–6'
Soil Temp. for Germ.: 60°–95°F
Sun: Full
Water: Moderate
Days to Germinate: 3–10
Days to Maturity: 80–105

### About Winter Squash

Remember, summer squash grows in the summer. So does winter squash. The name refers to how long it can be stored. Winter squash has a thick rind, which allows it to last through the winter. There are hundreds of varieties available, from acorn, pumpkin, and Hubbard types to butternut and turban cultivars. Winter squash can be cooked, roasted, or pureed, and is commonly used in soups, stews, and pies.

### Growing Winter Squash

Like summer squash, winter squash needs room to ramble. Give plants 3–6' of space. Early in the growing season, quick crops such as radishes and arugula can be grown in the surrounding soil, then harvested before the squash takes over. Plant the seeds in well-amended soil on mounds or hills (see Summer Squash for sandy soil alternatives). Plant the seeds in a triangle (a few seeds in each hole) and thin to the strongest plants once they develop several sets of leaves. Like summer squash, winter squash is aided by hand pollination. Keep it watered to prevent wilting.

### Harvesting Winter Squash

Winter squash is easy to harvest; just wait until the foliage dies back and cut off the stem, leaving at least 1" of stem attached (squash stores better that way). Some gardeners leave their harvest out in the sun for a few days to cure before storing.

### Common Problems

See Summer Squash for pests and powdery mildew solutions.

## Tomatoes

Latin Name: *Lycopersicon esculentum*
Planting Depth: ¼"
Plant Spacing: 12–18"
Soil Temp. for Germ.: 70°–90°F
Sun: Full
Water: Moderate
Days to Germinate: 6–10
Days to Maturity: 70–80

### About Tomatoes

Technically a fruit, tomatoes are the most popular garden crop in America. Curiously, they were considered poisonous until 1820, when Colonel Robert Gibbon Johnson ate them on the courthouse steps in Salem, New Jersey, to prove a point. There is nothing like a homegrown tomato, because most gardeners can grow varieties that wouldn't survive in market conditions. Tomatoes behave as perennials but are grown as annuals in the warm/hot season because a killing frost will put an end to most tomato plants. They are available as determinate, producing all fruit at once, or indeterminate, meaning they produce fruit over an extended period of time.

### Growing Tomatoes

Start from seed indoors in late winter or buy transplants from reliable sources in spring. Plant outside after threat of frost has passed. Mix in a handful of Epsom salts in the bottom of the planting hole to help prevent blossom-end rot (see Common Problems). Apply compost tea or vegetable fertilizer when transplanting the plants. Fertilize them again after first tomatoes set fruit and are about 1" in diameter. Apply fertilizer again after a month or so to keep production going. Most people water their tomatoes too much. Once established, water them deeply once per week (in ground, but more if in containers). Once they set fruit, water them deeply every ten days. This encourages roots to dive deep for water. For more detailed information about planting tomatoes, see Homemade Tomato Cages: How to Build a Tomato Crib (Chapter 8).

### Harvesting Tomatoes

To know when a tomato is ready to pick, cup it between your thumb and two fingers and rock the tomato back and forth, away from you. A ripe tomato should release from the vine easily. If you have to pull, it's not ready; check back tomorrow. If a killing frost is on its way, harvest all green mature fruit and either wrap each tomato individually in newspaper to ripen over the next several weeks or make fried green tomatoes. Some tomatoes will continue to survive and ripen in winter if laid down and covered with insulated garden fabric.

### Common Problems

Tomato hornworms are fat, green caterpillars with white stripes on the body, and a signature horn/tail. They eat all parts of a tomato in no time. It's best to handpick them off if you can find them (they are well disguised). Hornworms can be parasitized by broconid wasps (*Cotesia congregates*), while ladybugs, lacewings, and paper wasps eat hornworm young.

Fungal diseases like verticillium and Fusarium wilts, early and late blight, and septoria leaf spot damage leaves and fruit, and can even kill a tomato plant entirely. These diseases remain in the soil, so crop rotation is very important.

Blossom-end rot appears as a brown mushy patch on the bottom of tomatoes. It is caused by both a calcium deficiency and irregular soil moisture. It can be prevented with Epsom salts.

# Herbs

## Basil

Latin Name: *Ocimum basilicum*
Planting Depth: ⅛–¼"
Plant Spacing: 6"
Soil Temp. for Germ.: 70°–85°F
Sun: Full
Water: Moderate
Days to Germinate: 6–12
Days to Maturity: 65–75

### About Basil

Basil is the quintessential summer herb. Its leaves are used in salads, Italian cooking, pesto (see Chapter 10), Caprese sandwiches, and more. It is a member of the mint family, but it doesn't take over gardens as mint does. There are many basil varieties available, including Thai, lemon, Big Leaf, Lettuce, and even a few perennial basils such as African Blue and Pesto Perpetuo.

### Growing Basil

Sow the seeds in well-amended, loose soil. Basil can be fussy, so start the plants indoors in spring in cold climates. Water them regularly to keep the seed bed moist and roots cool as the plants develop. Basil will grow more quickly once temperatures warm up. Pinch flowering tips off to keep the plants producing through summer and fall.

### Harvesting Basil

Harvest the topmost leaves by picking individual leaves or leaf sets. You'll see two sets of small leaves growing from the nodes along the stem. Pinch the stems with your fingernails or shears just above new growth. Basil can be used fresh, frozen, or dried. Home-dried and frozen basil isn't pretty—it turns black—but it tastes the same in cooked dishes. Freeze basil in ice cube trays in tablespoon-serving amounts, or puree it with olive oil and freeze. For best results, dry basil in a dehydrator.

## Chives

Latin Name: *Allium schoenoprasum*
Planting Depth: ¼"
Plant Spacing: 12"
Soil Temp. for Germ.: 45°–95°F
Sun: Full to partial
Water: Moderate
Days to Germinate: 7–21
Days to Maturity: 60–70

### About Chives

Chives are a perennial herb of Mediterranean origin, related to the onion. They grow in clumps about 10" tall and spread in diameter as they mature. Typically used in egg dishes and Asian food, chives produce a pink spherical flower that is also edible. Another common variety, garlic or Chinese chives (*Allium tuberosum*), has broad, flat leaves with a seam down the center. Even though they have a different flavor, chives are a great alternative for those with little space to grow full-sized onions.

### Growing Chives

Chives can be grown from seed or nursery stock, or by dividing an existing plant. Start the plants indoors or direct seed in the garden, but note that chives can take up to a year to reach mature size. In warm-winter climates chives will survive through winter, but they go dormant in cold-winter zones. Water regularly until they are well established, then chives become somewhat drought tolerant. This herb grows well in partial shade. Fertilize them seasonally, as needed.

### Harvesting Chives

Cut the chives from the base of the plant, taking small sections each time. Chives will not grow from the cut end but will send up new shoots from the base. Harvesting encourages new growth. Store them in a plastic bag or in a glass of water like flowers in a vase.

## Cilantro

Latin Name: *Coriandrum sativum*
Planting Depth: ¼–½"
Plant Spacing: 4"
Soil Temp. for Germ.: 55°–65°F
Sun: Full
Water: Moderate
Days to Germinate: 7–14
Days to Maturity: 45–70

### About Cilantro

Cilantro is one of those annual herbs people either love or hate. There are some folks who think it tastes like soap. It's not your fault, it's the aldehydes—fat molecules that also happen to be found in soaps, lotions, and yes, even some bugs. For those who love cilantro, you'll enjoy the fact that it has antibacterial properties that reportedly help fight off salmonella and other food-borne illnesses. Cilantro is one of the easiest herbs to grow (especially in the cool season) and produces prolific harvests over several months.

### Growing Cilantro

Plant cilantro in full sun in early spring or fall, but for best results in hot summer climates, tuck it behind something taller to give it a little shade. Cilantro bolts to seed quickly, so shade cloth or strategic planting behind taller crops will help prolong the plant's life. According to the University of Massachusetts, Amherst, Center for Agriculture, "The 'seed' of cilantro is actually the whole fruit with two embryos inside. This means that if you plant 10 'seeds' and get 100% germination you will have 20 cilantro plants." Cilantro can be started indoors or direct seeded in the garden. When cilantro bolts to seed, the flowers are part of a group of umbels that will attract beneficial insects to your garden. Water regularly, but don't let cilantro get wet feet.

### Harvesting Cilantro

Cilantro can be harvested as soon as the plant has about eight sets of leaves. Pick the outside leaves and the plant will keep producing from the center. If you want coriander for your spice collection, allow several plants to bolt to seed (heirloom or open-pollinated varieties only if you plan to grow those seeds) and stop watering to let the plant dry out completely. Green seeds form and turn brown, then can be harvested by cutting off stems and rubbing them between your hands to release the seeds into a paper bag or container. Winnow or sift away the chaff and store the seeds in an envelope or jar in a cool, dry place. Lazy (or smart) gardeners let cilantro seeds fall in the garden to reseed themselves next season.

## Oregano

Latin Name: *Origanum vulgare*
Planting Depth: ⅛"
Plant Spacing: 12"
Soil Temp. for Germ.: 60°–80°F
Sun: Full to partial
Water: Moderate
Days to Germinate: 5–10
Days to Maturity: 60–80

### About Oregano

Culinary oregano is a classic perennial herb found in many Mediterranean and Latin American dishes. It can be used fresh or dried and blends well with other herbs. The most common variety available at nurseries is "Greek" oregano, but a spicy oregano called "Mexican" (*Lippia graveolens*) is becoming more available as well.

### Growing Oregano

As a woody herb, oregano is best propagated from cuttings, or purchased as a transplant at a nursery. Those of you with plenty of patience, feel free to seed it indoors at home, following package directions. Oregano is a spreading herb that trails along the ground, making it a great groundcover for low-traffic areas, and ideal for spilling out of containers. Its flowers attract beneficial insects, and can be eaten (the flowers, not the insects). Oregano doesn't require heavy nutrients to grow, but it prefers well-drained soil.

### Harvesting Oregano

Oregano sends up new growth from the base of the plant, so snip off stems near the soil line as needed once they grow to 4–5" long. Oregano tends to get leggy if left alone, and once it flowers, the whole plant can be cut back to expose new, shorter growth. Some prefer to prune often to prevent oregano from flowering, since the plant oils reportedly lose potency once flowers develop.

### Common Problems

Spider mites can muddle the appearance of oregano's leaves, and aphids will attack a struggling plant. Use a hose to "wash" the plants regularly and inspect for infestations. Organic soap sprays or horticultural oils can be used as a last resort.

## Parsley

Latin Name: *Petroselinium crispum*
Planting Depth: ¼"
Plant Spacing: 5–12"
Soil Temp. for Germ.: 60°–80°F
Sun: Full to partial
Water: Moderate
Days to Germinate: 14–21
Days to Maturity: 75–85

### About Parsley

Parsley is a leafy biennial herb that is used to flavor and decorate dishes of all cuisines. There are several varieties commonly available, curly and Italian flat leaf being the most popular. Parsley is grown as an annual in warm climates because it tends to bolt to seed after one hot season. In cooler climates, you may be able to coax another year out of the plants. Parsley flowers are umbels, which attract beneficial insects to the garden. Once the plant flowers, however, the leaves are generally too strong to use.

### Growing Parsley

Parsley can be started from seed, but can take several weeks to germinate. For this reason, many gardeners prefer to use nursery stock. If you do want to start from seed, try soaking the seeds overnight in the refrigerator for better germination. Start seeds indoors in late winter or early spring. Nursery stock can be planted in fall in warm-winter climates. Parsley prefers well-amended soil and mid-season fertilizing as needed.

### Harvesting Parsley

Parsley can be harvested as soon as the plant has about eight sets of leaves. Pick the outside leaves and the plant will keep producing from the center. Leave enough leaves to maintain photosynthesis and generate new growth.

### Common Problems

Parsley is often the target for the parsley caterpillar, or what becomes a swallowtail butterfly. If possible, relocate these critters, or leave them be to let them become adult butterflies. See Oregano for treatment of spider mites and aphids. Occasionally, parsley can be afflicted with a mosaic virus. Pull and destroy the plant.

## Sage

Latin Name: *Salvia officinalis*
Planting Depth: ⅛"
Plant Spacing: 12–18"
Soil Temp. for Germ.: 60°–70°F
Sun: Full
Water: Moderate to Low
Days to Germinate: 10–21
Days to Maturity: 14–21

### About Sage

Culinary sage is just one of many varieties of sage available in the plant world. It belongs to the genus Salvia, which extends to nonedible and drought-tolerant plants that grow well in Mediterranean climates. It is a woody perennial with leaves that add earthy balance and flavor to winter squash dishes. Gardeners can grow gray, purple, or variegated sages to add color to the garden.

### Growing Sage

While sage can be grown from seed, it is best propagated from cuttings or plant division. It prefers a sunny location with well-drained or even sandy soil. It is a drought-tolerant plant, but once established it enjoys a deep watering every couple of months and benefits from an occasional foliar feeding of compost tea. Plant nursery stock in the spring, or fall in warm-winter climates, where sage overwinters well. It grows well in containers, but small pots may need additional watering.

### Harvesting Sage

Sage can be harvested leaf by leaf as needed. Cut just above a leaf node if you're using a whole stem. It's a good idea to leave several stems to ensure new growth will continue. Use sage fresh or dry it by hanging or laying it on paper towels. It can be crumbled or "rubbed" and stored in glass jars for later use.

## Thyme

Latin Name: *Thymus vulgaris*
Planting Depth: 1⁄16–1⁄8"
Plant Spacing: 6–12"
Soil Temp. for Germ.: 60°–70°F
Sun: Full to partial
Water: Moderate
Days to Germinate: 21–28
Days to Maturity: 180–240

### About Thyme

Thyme is another classic, perennial, woody herb used in Mediterranean cooking. Nurseries carry an assortment of varieties, including lemon, English, French, creeping and woolly (for groundcover), variegated, and common thyme. Thyme oil is used medicinally and in teas to resolve a number of ailments.

### Growing Thyme

Like other woody herbs, thyme is best propagated from cuttings or division mainly because it can take a long time for seeds to germinate, and for plants to mature. It prefers full sun, but can tolerate some shade. It doesn't require rich soil, but needs good drainage, as it doesn't like wet feet.

### Harvesting Thyme

Once established, thyme can be harvested as needed. The plant grows from the cut end, so to ensure a compact plant, give thyme a haircut several times per year by cutting back at least a third of the growth. Blossoms attract beneficial insects to the garden and can be tossed into salads (again, the blossoms, not the insects).

### Common Problems

See Oregano for treatment of spider mites and aphids. Ants find thyme to be a favorite place to build a nest. In wet conditions, roots can rot and plants can develop mold. Keep well drained and check regularly for ants. Borax-based ant traps are the closest thing to organic controls for ants. Use in situations of extreme infestation.

# CHAPTER 7

# IRRIGATION

It's simple: If vegetable crops and young fruit trees don't have water, they die. Conversely, most plants will thrive if you simply water them. Sure, fertilization, sun exposure, and pest management are all part of tending a garden, but without water, there's no vegetable garden to tend. With climate change and desertification happening all over the world, water is becoming scarce in places that need it most.

For example, in recent years central California farms have been severely affected by drought. Many farmers left acres of land uncultivated because water rations were too tight. Does our farming industry use the most efficient irrigation methods possible? If you drive along California's Highway 5 at noon on 100°F days you will see overhead sprinklers going off.

We home gardeners are fortunate. We don't have to shell out thousands of dollars for miles of drip tubing. With very little effort, we can easily design and install efficient irrigation systems for our little patches of land.

There are many ways to approach this task, depending on the philosophy to which you subscribe. There are ancient techniques to sequester water in soils, rainwater catchment systems, in-ground PVC sprinklers, above-ground drip systems, gray-water systems, and good old-fashioned hand watering. Let's explore some different approaches to giving your garden the moisture it needs.

## Hand Watering

If you want to live the simple life, with low-tech solutions for watering your garden, nothing beats a watering can or a garden hose with a good-quality spray nozzle. Watering tools are widely available from bargain-basement to high-end models, so it's good to know what to look for when you're shopping. Let's consider the options.

### Watering Cans

A good watering can has two handles, one on top and one opposite the spout. That makes it easier to carry and pour. A good can also holds enough water so you don't have to run back to your water source frequently. A two-gallon watering can is light enough to carry when full, but will still hold a sufficient amount of water for the job.

The spout on a watering can should have a good rose on the end. The smaller the holes in the rose, the finer the delivery of water. The goal is to mimic rainfall, allowing soils to absorb moisture at a slow rate rather than pooling on the surface, so pinholes are best. The rose should be removable, so you can clear out leaves and other gunk that collect at the bottom of the can.

While those galvanized metal watering cans are beautiful, avoid them. Not only are they heavy and cumbersome, but they are coated with zinc, which can leach into the water and remain in the soil, locking up nutrients from plants. Haws, a British company that has been making watering cans since 1886, makes a terrific product that fulfills all of these criteria. Their six-liter Practican is the envy of many a gardener. Check out their website at *www.hawswateringcans.com.*

## Garden Hoses

Garden hoses have become more complicated as plastics have evolved. We were once limited to standard green garden hoses that kinked and split, but now there are a plethora of options for home gardeners, including coil hoses; kink-free, drinking-water-safe hoses; and hose color choices in every hue of the rainbow. There are even coil hoses that come with adapters to connect to your kitchen sink, in case you don't have access to a hose spigot outside.

Back up a second. Drinking-water safe? *"Aren't all hoses drinking-water safe?"* you ask as you think back to your childhood, slurping from the sprinkler nozzle on a hot summer day. Definitely not. Most hoses are made from polyvinyl chloride. As it happens, lead is used as a stabilizer when working with polyvinyl chloride, and there it remains until you use the hose to water your plants. According to *Consumer Reports*, which did a study on drinking-water safe and regular hoses in 2003, between ten and 100 times the allowable levels of lead were found in samples from hoses not labeled as drinking-water safe. The report recommends flushing the water from the hose first before using it each time. Another organization, HealthyStuff.org (*www.healthystuff.org*), sampled 179 garden products in 2012 and found more than 30 percent of the products contained lead in levels that exceeded allowable amounts for children's products. They also found traces of BPA (Bisphenol A) and phthalates. It wasn't just hoses—these chemicals were found in garden gloves, kneeling pads, and tools. It pays to do your research, garden geeks. Look for labeling that ensures what you buy is drinking-water safe.

A word about coil hoses. They can be great because you don't have to wind them up at the end of the day, but they can be annoying because once they tangle, it's challenging to restore order to the mess. Here's a hint—opt for coil hoses that are ⅝" in diameter rather than ½". The thicker diameter prevents the hose from twisting into itself as much. Newer coil hoses are even thinner—⅜" in diameter. Stay away from these hoses with smaller diameters.

## Hose Nozzles

Watering your garden is much easier if you have a spray nozzle attached to the end of your hose. While one can certainly admire the art of thumb-over-the-hose-end techniques, your seedlings will appreciate the gentle, even spray a nozzle can provide. Your housemates will also thank you for a lower water bill. Sprayer nozzles keep water from flowing from the hose until you need it, and many offer different settings for all of your gardening tasks. Use the "mist" setting on newly planted seeds or seedlings,

Water beading up on Orach mountain spinach.

"shower" for everyday watering that mimics rainfall, and "jet" for blasting bugs and cobwebs from infested trees and plants.

As product manufacturing migrated to other countries, the quality (and price!) of spray nozzles notably decreased, but there are still good-quality sprayers available. The key is to find one made from metal, not plastic. Plastic sprayers break down in less than a year, but metal sprayers hold up much longer. The only exception to this is a fan sprayer. Those classic yellow Y-shaped sprayers are the cheapest things around, and for some reason, they work better than some expensive nozzles. The crew at Ecology Action uses them because they mimic rainfall very well and are inexpensive, an important feature for thrifty gardeners who follow GROW BIO-INTENSIVE methods. You can prolong a sprayer's life by soaking the head in vinegar to remove hard water deposits. Try that before buying a new one. For a little more excitement, add baking soda and watch the bubbling action eat away at deposits.

If you plan to water by hand, keep in mind there are optimal times to do it. Mornings before nine and afternoons after four are best. In sunnier, hotter parts of the day, water will evaporate before your plants have a chance to absorb it. On really hot days during midday hours, plants can be scorched by overhead watering. Water acts as a magnifying glass to focus the sun's energy and heat on plant leaves, so you may find your entire garden burned to a crisp the day after an early afternoon bout with a hose. There are differing schools of thought about when to water. Some experts emphatically recommend watering only in the morning, because evening watering can lead to mildew or rot. Experts on the other side of the fence firmly believe that we should only water in late afternoon, so plants can use the moisture overnight to grow. It really depends on your climate. If you live in an area that is humid or shrouded by marine layer, watering in the morning might be the best thing to allow plant leaves to dry out before the clouds roll in later in the day. For those with hot, dry days, watering at night will ensure a longer period of access to moisture without threat of evaporation. The bottom line is to see what works for you.

Some gardeners prefer to drizzle water at the soil level with a bucket and cup, or they fill up water bottles and connect them to special cones that sit below ground to deliver the water at the root level. The Native Americans were introduced to Spanish ollas, which came to Spain from Africa, as a method for watering underground. Ollas are unglazed jugs with long necks that are buried in the ground, leaving only the jug's open mouth exposed. Gardeners fill the jugs with water, which seeps through porous walls into the soil right where the roots need it. Water seeps to about 9" out from the jugs, so plants don't need to be right next to them. Ollas are still used today in gardens to conserve water.

## Drip Irrigation

Some claim drip irrigation is the ultimate obsession for garden geeks. It's all about coming up with the coolest, most clever system that is completely invisible, and uses the least amount of water with no overspray. Just a quick walk down the garden plumbing aisle at the hardware store will give you a sense of just how many possibilities there are for aboveground irrigation: ½" tubing, ¼" tubing, tubing with or without emitters, and soaker hoses that sweat. Then there's the array of emitters to choose from: spider bubblers, flag emitters, inline flow emitters, pressure-compensating emitters, micro-sprayers, micro-sprinklers, micro-sprayers with flow control valves, and even fogger/mister attachments. Oh, the possibilities!

¼" drip tubing with a tee connector used for irrigating a vertical garden system.

Think of drip irrigation like a Lego Ultimate Building Set. All the pieces fit together in a hundred different combinations. Some pieces are specialized, but there is logic to how they fit together. You have tubing attached to connectors, which connect to more tubing. Good-quality connectors are usually barbed so they hold in place better, and can be straight (inline), elbows, or tees. There are also plugs called end caps to close off the tubes, and even plugs called goof plugs (no lie) for patching up holes you didn't mean to make.

To connect the tubing to a water source, there are a few other parts to consider. First, a timer is connected to the hose spigot to control the frequency and duration of water flow. Next is a series of backflow preventers, filters, and pressure regulators that screw together and eventually end with a connection to the drip tubing that will inevitably reach your garden. Not all of these parts are necessary in every situation. It depends on your water source, the size of your system, and how much you are willing to invest.

For a small and simple system, a gardener might disregard the need for a filter or a pressure regulator. If you have control over your hose spigot, and leave it turned on in the same place all the time, chances are you won't have enough variance in water pressure to burst the tubing. And given that most timers come with a screen filter on both ends, in many cases they eliminate the need for a flushable filter. However, if you are attaching drip irrigation to an underground sprinkler system, don't skimp on the pressure regulator or filter. The extra expense is worth not having to dig the whole thing up later on.

A battery-operated timer connected to ¼" drip tubing with an adapter.

## Water: How Much/How Often

When it comes to irrigation, soil behaves like a sponge. Have you ever tried to wipe up a spill with a dry sponge? Rather than absorb the spill, it just pushes it around. Soil does the same thing when it's very dry. You may have to slowly wet the soil for a few days before it can absorb water, just as you have to wet a sponge thoroughly and squeeze it out before it can sop up a mess. Keeping soil moisture consistent will help you water less each time you irrigate, because it will penetrate properly. A layer of mulch will help retain moisture.

For hand watering, start with a gentle setting on your sprayer nozzle and be patient. If water starts to pool up, turn the hose down or pause for a minute. Watch for what John Jeavons calls "the shiny." It's that moment where water soaks into the soil and glistens on the surface for about one or two seconds as it sinks down. Once you achieve "the shiny" repeat the process until the area is thoroughly irrigated.

When using drip irrigation, it's a good idea to know just how much water is being delivered to your garden. Some cities have laws requiring drip systems to operate efficiently, below a maximum "inches per hour" flow rate. Russell Ackerman, the water resource specialist for the City of Santa Monica, California is an expert in drip irrigation math, and his formula for calculating drip system precipitation rates is too geeky to resist. Put on your math caps as you read through his calculations.

### Calculation of Precipitation Rate (PR) of Drip Emitters . . . by Russell Ackerman, CLIA-D

Water typically infiltrates into soil at a rate of ¾" per hour or less. By slowing the rate at which water is applied to a landscape, we can prevent runoff and allow water to percolate through the soil, down to the plant roots where it's needed.

**Precipitation Rate (PR)**—The rate at which water is applied to a landscape area by an irrigation system or watering device measured in *inches per hour*.

**Total Root Area**—The total square footage of soil above the mature root systems of all *irrigated* plants in the zone.

**Total Zone GPM**—The total amount of water applied by all the emitters in the zone in gallons per *minute*.

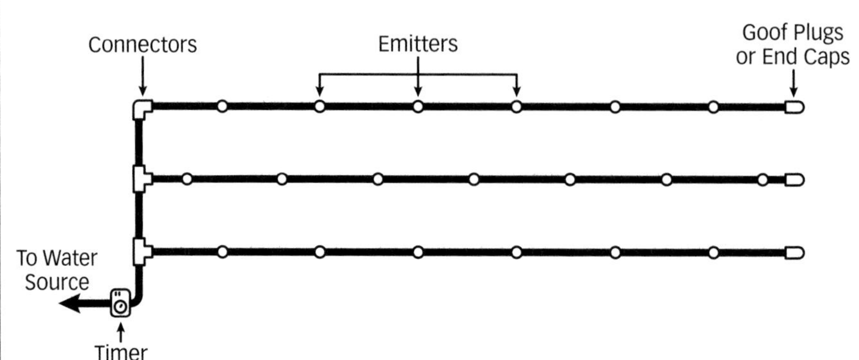


**A reliable drip system using ½" tubing, tee connectors, and end caps (use goof plugs for ¼" tubing).**

**GPH**—Gallons per hour (÷ 60 min/hr to get gallons per minute)
*Author's note: Drip tubing is rated by gallons per hour, so a product that says 0.5 indicates the emitter flow rate is 0.05 GPH.*
**231.1**—A conversion factor that converts gallon/hour to cubic inches/hour . . .

**Formula:** PR = (231.1 × Emitter Flow Rate *in GPH*) ÷ (Emitter Spacing *in inches* × Row Spacing *in inches*)

**Example:** Backyard with rows of Rain Bird XF 0.5 × 12" tubing spaced 15" apart.

(231.1 × 0.5) ÷ (12 × 15) = 115.6 ÷ 180 = 0.64 in/hr 0.64 < 0.75 in/hr = good!

Even with nifty rule-of-thumb formulas, though, irrigation is not an exact science. A lot depends on your soil structure and the types of plants you are growing. That's why most watering instructions for vegetables are vague. They read, "requires moderate water," or "let soil dry out between waterings." Remember, clay soil will hold water longer than sandy soil. Seeds and seedlings will probably need water every day until root systems develop. Once plants grow in and form a living mulch over the soil (or you add a mulch layer), less water is needed. In the end, your soil and plants will tell you if they are getting enough water. You can use the Two-Knuckle Test (see sidebar) to monitor your soil's moisture level.

Plants have their way of sending signals about moisture too. Plants wilt or change color when something is wrong. If a plant turns brown and crisp, that usually means it didn't get enough water. If it turns yellow, that usually means its roots are suffocating from too much water—not enough oxygen in the soil. Yellow can also mean your plants need nitrogen, so if cutting back water doesn't solve the problem, perform a soil test to determine nutrient deficiencies.

If you see your plants wilting during the warmest, sunniest part of the day, resist the urge to throw water on them immediately, unless they are new transplants. Instead, wait until late afternoon and inspect the plants again. If they are still wilted after direct sunlight has passed, they need water. Some plants, like tomatoes, have a defense mechanism to curl up during the hot part of the day. They perk back up after sunset like nothing was ever wrong. Don't be fooled.

Given that your situation is going to be unique and you will learn about your garden's irrigation needs through trial and error, here is a less-vague suggestion for watering a typical raised bed vegetable garden: Set your drip timer for three days per week for 10–15 minutes. You can hand water newly planted seeds and seedlings on the off days to ensure the seed beds stay consistently moist. Reduce the days per week during rainy season as needed, and shut irrigation off completely on rainy days. Many timers are equipped with a rain delay setting.

### GEEKY GARDENING TIP

#### TWO-KNUCKLE TEST

Once again, the best way to know what's going on in your garden is to be in your garden. To test existing soil moisture, drill a hole in garden soil with your index finger past the second knuckle. Pull away some soil to see if it looks wet at the tip of your finger. If it's dry, it's time to water.

## Water Catchment: Rain Barrels, Gray Water, and Other Ways to Capture Water

If we're striving to be as sustainable as possible in our gardens, it makes sense to create ways to sequester water in the soil or utilize rainfall, rather than to pump it in from municipal sources. Since yearly rainfall varies from hardiness zone to hardiness zone, your need to capture water may be more important than it is for others. For example, upstate New York averages 40–50" of rain per year. Los Angeles gets only 12–15"—and that all happens over three or four months. So what's a person to do when it's not raining? Let's look at the options for water catchment.

One option for a rain barrel. Some cities sell them at a subsidized rate to residents.

## Rain Barrels

These containers are placed under the downspout of a rain gutter to funnel rainfall from the roof. The amount of water that can be collected this way is staggering, if you have room for enough rain barrels. Here's the formula:

(Area of roof in SF) × (Inches of rain/period) × (0.6 gallons/inch of rain/SF) × (0.75) = (Gallons/period)

First, calculate your surface area by multiplying the length and width of your roof in feet (including the gutters).

Next choose a number for inches of rain per period you want to capture and store it. For simplicity, let's assume the period we're interested in is one day. The average daily rainfall in your hardiness zone can be found on just about any weather website. For simplicity, let's choose 1" of rainfall per day.

The next number (0.6) represents the standard number of gallons of water that can be collected for every inch of rain, for every 1000 square feet of roof.

The number 0.75 is a rule-of-thumb efficiency coefficient for collecting roof water. Think of this as the margin of error, or nature's way of keeping some of the harvest. This number will vary from climate to climate, and from roof to roof, but 0.75 is a good starting point.

Now you have the number of gallons per day you can collect from your roof with 1" of rainfall per day. Or, if you prefer, this is the number of gallons you can collect from your roof with 1" of rainfall over a period of time.

Another option for a rain barrel.

Example:

(20' L × 40' W) × (1"/day) × (0.6 gal/inches of rain/SF) × (0.75) =

(800 square feet) × (1" of rain/day) × (0.6 gal/inches of rain/SF) × (0.75 efficiency) = 360 gallons/day

That's a lot of water from 1" of rain. Most rain barrels hold fifty-five or sixty gallons, so you would need six or seven of them to contain the storm water. (Here's a money saving tip: your municipal green waste bin holds about ninety gallons, and if you're composting most of your green waste, you can use the bin all winter for water catchment.) There are above-ground cisterns on the market that hold between 300–10,000 gallons. Some gardeners have several rain barrels, each under a downspout at different corners of the house. The downspouts usually need to be cut shorter to spill into the top of the rain barrel. You can connect overflow hoses to fill up additional barrels if you have room.

If rain is infrequent, you will be able to use up the contents of your rain barrel before the next rain. Some gardeners in low-rainfall areas have been able to turn off their irrigation completely for six months through the use of water catchment in just three rain barrels. Another tip for garden safety: don't collect the first rain of the season, or the first day if it hasn't rained in a while. Oils and other pollutants will wash off the roof. You don't want that in your garden, so wait a day to divert water to your rain barrels.

## Gray Water Systems

Recycling gray water from household appliances is a touchy subject. For years it has been illegal in many cities and states, but laws are changing as water shortages populate headlines. Gray water systems can be as simple as placing a bucket in the shower while the water warms up, or as complex as having a diverter to redirect washing machine water to a tank or flower bed. What's important to remember is if you plan to use gray water, you have to use biodegradable soaps and detergents. There is much debate over whether gray water can be used to water vegetable gardens, and this book will not attempt to sort out that issue.

According to a "white paper" report from the WateReuse Association, the average household generates thirty-nine gallons of gray water per day from washing clothes and taking showers or baths (gray water typically does not include water from the toilet, dishwasher, or kitchen sink). That's two-thirds of a rain barrel. If you could redirect even part of that waste water to flower beds or lawns, you could save precious dollars (not to mention gallons) per year. Check your city ordinances to find out about the laws for gray water systems in your area. There are DIY books or local professionals who can help. Just make sure you have a plan before you start redirecting plumbing on your own.

### Swales

Before the invention of drip tape and sprinkler systems, farm cultures directed water through strategically placed channels to irrigate farmlands. Nature makes its own channels in forests and plains, carving out paths for snowmelt to trickle toward rivers. Along the way, plants benefit from water that is absorbed deep into the soil to be drawn upon later in the dry season. Such is the nature of a swale. Swales (pronounced like tails) are shallow trenches that not only funnel water along a path but also help sequester water in underground stores for deep roots to access later on. Permaculturists mimic nature by contouring the soil of a garden to direct water where it is most needed. On hillsides where water might ordinarily run downhill, causing erosion, a swale running across the hillside can stop water in its path and trap it underground near crops or fruit trees.

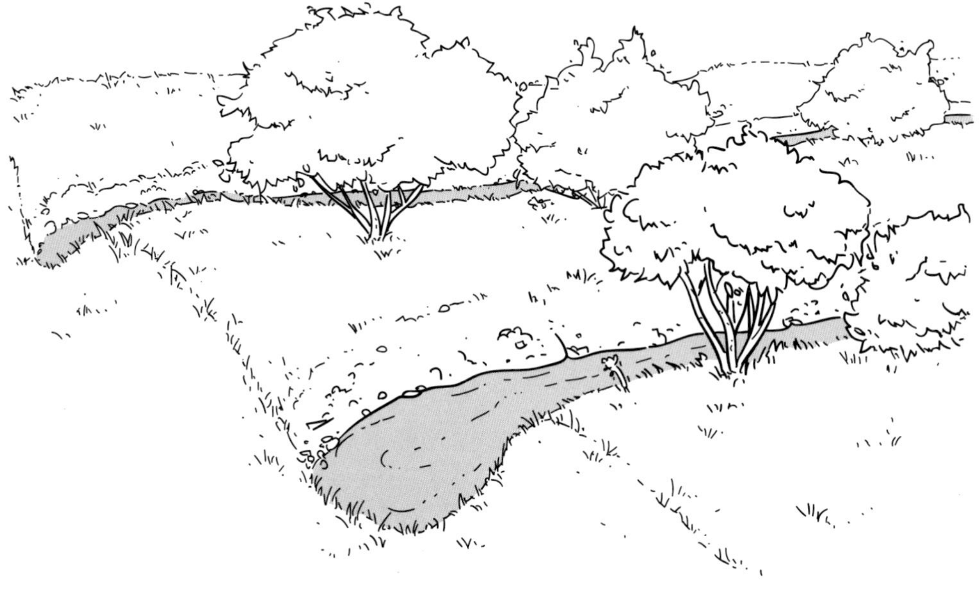

**Swales situated on the high side of a slope help sequester water for trees below.**

Keeping water on site will likely make your garden better. These water-capturing techniques each merit more investigation to learn their subtleties, but as a good garden geek that shouldn't be much of a problem for you.

# EVO FARM: A FIELD TRIP TO AN AQUAPONICS FARM

Aquaponics is a combination of hydroponics and aquaculture. Instead of using soil, it uses a nearly closed-loop system of aquariums (or aquaria if we're going to use proper Latin) of fish to produce the nutrient fertilizer for plants to feed upon. Plants grow through rafts that float atop the water, which is infused with fish droppings and is filtered for solids. Through a complex system of pipes, the water recycles back through the system to the fish and the whole process starts all over again.

It is a cool October morning at EVO Farm, a Los Angeles–based experimental growing grounds that combines yard-sharing with aquaponics. The creators of EVO Farm didn't have their own space to experiment, so they found neighbors with extra space in their yard who were excited about the idea of picking fresh produce from a garden they didn't have to tend themselves.

The greenhouse is located on a double lot, with rows of two-tiered garden "beds" made from steel and CFC-free Styrofoam. The greenhouse allows for a controlled environment with walls that roll up in hot weather. David Rosenstein, one of the two founders of EVO Farm, explains the features of the farm.

The "beds" are filled with water rather than soil. The floating foam rafts have uniform holes, each filled with coir and vegetable crops. David lifts a lettuce raft to expose hundreds of vibrant white roots sprawling happily down into the water below. He explains that because of this method and the high-quality nutrients the fish provide, the turnaround time from transplant to harvest is faster than in the ground.

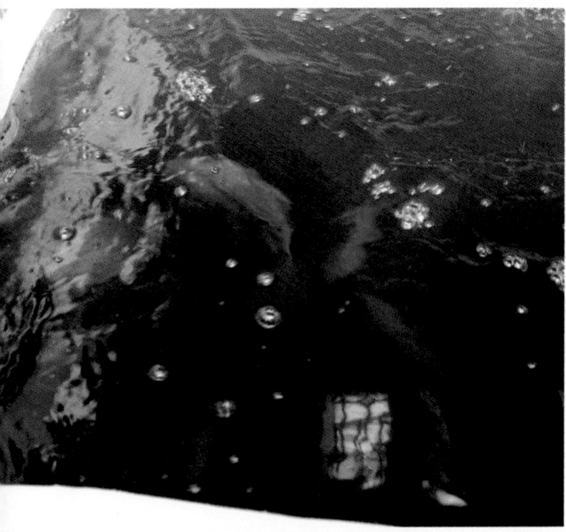

**Fish swimming in their recycled home.**

The whole thing starts with the fish. David lifts a plywood cover off a recycled 250-gallon dairy container (think enormous milk jug with the top cut off), which holds several dozen tilapia and catfish. It is one of two holding tanks that are in constant, gentle motion.

Along with beneficial algae and bacterial inputs, David adds fish food, and the fish gobble it up. As of 2012, there's no such thing as organic fish, but they hope to change this at EVO Farm. David's goal is to cultivate a truly sustainable, commercially viable fish food using a combination of insects and nitrogen-fixing aquatic plants; at that point he believes his fish would qualify to be called Certified Organic.

The water from the holding tanks goes through filters where the bacteria can colonize on some gravel media. The gravel provides "stacking functions": mechanical filtration, biological filtration, aeration, and growing space. David explains why bacteria are important to the process: "Beneficial bacteria live in the water that feed on ammonia and convert it from nitrites to nitrates. Nitrates are a direct food source for plants . . . i.e., liquid fertilizer!"

The result is amazingly fast, healthy growth of plants without soil. The lower tier of plants is mainly cool weather crops, since they get less sunlight than their neighbors upstairs. As it turns out, there is enough reflected light to keep them vibrant and strong. EVO Farm has a steady supply of new plants in the nursery—a three-tiered shelf unit lined with waterproof plastic. The farmers flood the deep shelves with the same water that cycles through the farm.

The founders of EVO Farm have big plans for expansion, including a new CSA (community supported agriculture) program that feeds local residents. They have also created an outreach program to build farms in schools, by partnering with several organizations within local school districts. Their first project is a 1.3-acre commercial farm on a school campus that includes aquaponics, food forests, and row crops. "Some of the harvest is consumed by students at school, some goes home with their parents, and the rest is sold to restaurants and other channels," David explains. "We hope to replicate this model at least 100 times." They also plan to harvest the fish for market—it will be organic, of course.

In order to set up the original test farm greenhouse, some existing landscaping had to be cleared. In keeping with EVO Farm's concept of recycling nutrients, it has all been composted for later use. David has plans to use the compost bins outside the greenhouse to provide heat for the building and water system during winter. Visit EVO Farm's website at *www.evofarm.com* for more details about how aquaponics works.

Seedling trays are part of the virtually closed-loop system.

# CHAPTER 8

# KEEPING ORDER: TRELLISES AND CAGES FOR CROPS

While geekdom and OCD often go hand in hand, being a garden geek doesn't necessarily mean you are orderly by nature. In fact, many garden geeks prefer meandering, sprawling garden jungles rather than color-inside-the-lines, pruned-to-perfection gardens. Wherever you fall on the spectrum of order, it's important to remember that vegetables—just like people—grow better if they are well supported.

Choosing the right trellis for a plant can make the difference between success and failure. If you grow peas on a 4' trellis, you will find out the hard way that peas easily grow to a height of 8–10'. Without something sturdy to climb, stems can snap or crease as they collapse, shortening the plants' productivity and lifespan. This chapter reviews the various and sundry selections of trellising contraptions for tall and vining crops.

## Materials for Trellises and Cages

There are as many ways to support a crop as there are crop varieties themselves. Tomato cages alone come in a blinding array of sizes, shapes, and colors. Many gardeners prefer to have a multipurpose trellis that works for peas, cucumbers, pole beans, melons, and tomatoes. To fit the bill, you may have to build the support structure of your dreams, but there are also commercial options available. Let's look at the practicality of different trellis materials.

### Wood

If you want to build an A-frame permanent trellis in part of your garden, 2' × 4' lumber should do the trick. While conventional wisdom would say to use pressure-treated lumber, it is not recommended for use around food crops. Instead, paint the bottom portions of the legs with several coats of latex paint and use cedar, redwood, or composite lumber to ensure durability.

Ready-made redwood trellises are available in heights ranging from 3–10', and usually have 7–8" grid openings. This allows gardeners to reach through to harvest and tame wild vines. Panels of redwood lattice can be used as a trellis, but do not have sufficient space for hands to get through. These panels need a solid framework in order to hold up heavy crops, so avoid panels that are sold without a wooden frame. Lattice is great for attaching to walls or fences.

Willow branches are a natural trellising option for those interested in picking up a new skill set that crosses over from gardening into folk art. The flexibility of willow makes it great for creating curved designs, arches, and even gates or furniture. There are several publications about the art, the most well known being *Making Bentwood Arbors and Trellises* by Jim Long. Plant a willow tree for a continuous supply of materials in the years to come; you'll also be able to weave your own harvest baskets.

### Metal

Half-inch galvanized pipe is a great starting point for a metal trellis. By creating a frame with two 10' vertical lengths hammered into the ground, and a cross bar

connected by elbow joints, you will have a trellis that will last upwards of ten years. Stretch mesh netting across the frame, or run twine in vertical lines down to the bed, and you'll have a versatile yet permanent trellis that will work for all sorts of climbing crops, including tomatoes.

Chain link fences make fine supports for vining crops, as do a lot of the folding metal cages and supports that are available commercially. For serious tomato growers, Texas Tomato Cages are the only thing that will do. They're 6' tall, 24" in diameter, and are made from ¼" galvanized steel. You won't be using bio-intensive plant spacing with these cages, but your tomatoes will be well supported.

Coated rebar is indispensible for bracing trellises in the wind, or for preventing tall crops from collapsing. Attach 8' rebar stakes on either side of wide, flat trellises for extra support on windy days. When pole beans overtake cornstalks, a common occurrence when growing a Three Sisters Garden, rebar stakes come in handy to prop up overbearing vines.

Grow-through supports are dainty, coated metal trellises for short crops, or plants that tend to sprawl open as they flower and age. They look like miniature tables with three or four legs and a lattice tabletop. Install them while plants are young; the shoots will grow right though the lattice and stay upright.

Thick-gauge wire is used for keeping blackberries and other cane berries in check. It can also be used with eye hooks to train grapevines and other climbing vines along a wall or fence.

### Bamboo

This renewable resource is strong and compostable, so if you want to take the natural approach to trellising, bamboo is an excellent choice. Some gardeners grow bamboo on site to have a constant supply. Bamboo can be lashed together to form A-frame trellises, or woven together to form a lattice. Teepees are typically constructed from bamboo by lashing three or four poles together on one end, and securing the other ends in the ground at an angle. Individual stakes can be sturdy enough for supporting determinate tomatoes and some wayward vines. Use stakes that are at least ¾" thick. Single stakes of any material are not recommended for indeterminate tomatoes, unless you don't mind having tomato vines all over the place. Use cages instead.

### Nylon and Other Plastics

Fishing line is often used to guide espaliered fruit trees or grapevines up a wall. Gardeners install eye hooks in strategic places and weave fishing line to provide places for vines to grab on to. The line is nearly invisible, and you can add more as needed.

Mesh netting is a great solution for trellising crops such as peas and others that tend to wander. Cover a sturdy trellis frame with a layer of 7" netting and watch vines cover it in no time. Bird netting, which has 1" mesh, will work for this task, though you can't get your hands through it to harvest crops on both sides.

## Which Plants to Trellis or Cage

Unwieldy plants come in all shapes and sizes, so there's more than one way to tackle the issue of supporting them. The following chart will help guide you toward the right kind of trellis for your behemoth blackberry or your arching asparagus. It also includes trailing crops that can be trellised for space efficiency.

Remember that when you use a trellis, most climbing plants will eventually grab on, but they require guidance at first until enough tendrils have a firm hold. Tomatoes don't have tendrils to grasp supports, so keep a watchful eye on new shoots that will attempt to escape the confines of a cage. Check plants often and gently guide shoots upright.

## Plant and Trellis Partnerships

| Plant Name | Ideal Trellis | Notes |
|---|---|---|
| Asparagus | 6' stakes in four corners, twine surrounding bed | Tie several levels to catch low and high branches. |
| Beans, pole | 8' sturdy metal frame covered with 7" netting | Bamboo teepees with twine around circumference works well. If growing with corn as a trellis, choose very tall corn varieties. |
| Blackberries/ Raspberries | 4' × 4' posts every 5' with 2' × 4' cross bars. Run 22-gauge wire through tips of cross bars to form outer supports for canes | |
| Cantaloupe (and other muskmelons) | Metal or wooden trellis with 7–8" grid spacing | Use old T-shirts or pantyhose to sling fruit to the trellis as it ripens. |
| Cucumbers | 8' sturdy metal frame covered with 7" netting | Lean-to style wood or metal lattice trellises allow cucumbers to grow while providing shade for lettuce crops beneath. |
| Fava Beans | 4–6' stakes in four corners, twine surrounding bed | Small groupings may be tied together loosely. |
| Grains | No trellis needed, but stakes can be used on top-heavy stalks before harvest | |
| Peas | 8' sturdy metal frame covered with 7" netting | Bamboo teepees with twine around circumference works well, or a wooden lattice. |
| Peppers | Grow-through plant supports or stakes with twist ties | Some peppers are fine without support. |
| Pumpkins | Metal or wooden trellis with 7–8" grid spacing | Use old T-shirts or pantyhose to sling fruit to the trellis as it ripens. |
| Summer Squash | Metal or wooden trellis with 7–8" grid spacing | Do not attempt to trellis bush varieties. |
| Tomatoes | Sturdy metal cage with 7–8" grid spacing | See further for how to make your own. |
| Watermelon | Metal or wooden trellis with 7–8" grid spacing | Use old T-shirts or pantyhose to sling fruit to the trellis as it ripens. |

# HOMEMADE TOMATO CAGES: HOW TO BUILD A TOMATO CRIB

What the heck is a tomato crib, you ask? Well, for starters, it involves breaking a rule—or, at any rate, a commonly held belief—about tomato growing. Most nurseries and gardening books will tell you that you have to space tomato plants 2–3' apart. This tomato crib allows you to grow four different varieties of tomatoes in 4 square feet of space, without wrestling with round, weak tomato cages. If you prepare your soil correctly, you will have a bounty of tomatoes that will have your neighbors either welcoming or dreading your knock on their door (depending on how much they like tomatoes).

After you've prepared your soil for planting (mixing in organic fertilizer for acid-loving plants, and plenty of compost because tomatoes are considered "heavy feeders," meaning they need a lot of nutrients to draw upon), follow these instructions:

First, let's plant your tomatoes. Mark out an area 1' wide × 4' long and divide the space into 4 square feet. Mark the center of each square foot. Dig a hole for each tomato plant that is twice as deep as the root ball. Snip or pinch off all the leaves from the base of the plant up to the level that is equal to a few inches above the surface of the hole you just dug. This will accomplish two things: deep roots mean strong plants, and trimming the leaves will keep water and soil from accumulating on your plant. Next, throw a handful of Epsom salts into each hole. This will help prevent blossom-end rot, a nasty disease that ruins otherwise perfectly good tomatoes, come harvest time. Mix that in a little and plant your tomato, backfilling it gently (don't push down; let watering do the work for you, then you can add more soil).

Now, once your tomatoes are planted, you will need a 10' length of concrete wire mesh (the kind that stands up on its own) that is 5' tall, with generous 6" × 6" grid spacing so you can get your hands through when harvesting.

Use wire cutters to cut the horizontals off one edge of the mesh to expose vertical spikes that will be your anchors that drive into the ground.

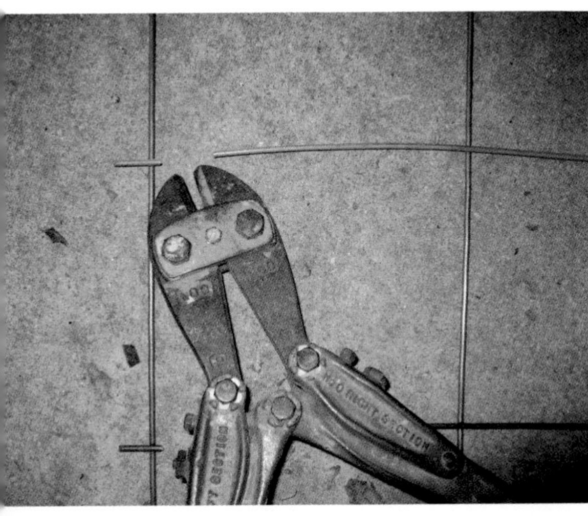

Next, it's time to make a 1' × 4' rectangular cage by making 90-degree folds in the width of the fencing at the 1' mark, the 5' mark, and the 9' mark. The photograph below shows the result.

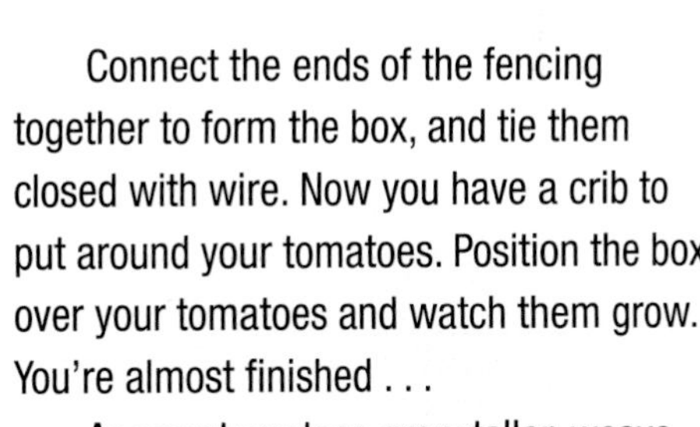

Connect the ends of the fencing together to form the box, and tie them closed with wire. Now you have a crib to put around your tomatoes. Position the box over your tomatoes and watch them grow. You're almost finished . . .

As your tomatoes grow taller, weave sturdy twine across the opening of the crib to create a grid for the tomatoes to grow through. Start by tying off the twine near a corner and run it across the cage to wrap it around the other end of the wire mesh.

Then take the twine to the next rung, wrap it once around that rung, and continue directly across to the other side. Continue running twine around each rung and across to the opposite side until you've covered the opening, then weave twine perpendicularly through to complete the grid.

Start near the bottom and work your way up. Usually you will want to add a new layer of twine per week as the tomatoes grow through the lower layers of twine. It only takes a few minutes to add a new layer. Within about a month, you will have created a three-dimensional lattice that cradles your tomato vines, and you won't have to worry about them for the rest of the summer.

See Appendix C for diagramed instructions to make a tomato crib that holds eight tomatoes (a 2' × 4' cage).

Tomato crib lattice: looking down into the inside of a tomato crib.

## Plant Wrangling: Basic Pruning Tips

It happens to everyone, though not all gardeners will admit it. At least once in a while, the garden gets out of control. You go on vacation or turn your back for, oh . . . a few weeks, and suddenly the tomato vines are 3' longer, the melons are trailing over every square inch of pathway, and the cane berries have taken over the back forty. Here are some basic tips for wrestling your vegetable and fruit crops back into compliance.

### The Three Ds: Dead, Diseased, and Disorderly

When things get out of hand, it helps to have a starting point—in this case, dead leaves, vines, and branches. Cut those away, and you will begin to see some space for a closer look. Diseased plant matter is easy to identify. It's wilted, brown or yellow, has spots, and basically looks terrible. Cut those away and toss them, but not in the compost bin, unless you run a hot bin that gets over 160°F (anything less will not kill weed seeds or diseases). Then we get to disorderly. This means branches that are crossing, vines that have fallen away from trellises, congested berry canes, or annuals that have gone to seed. Where to start? Here are some suggestions.

#### Be Ruthless

If it won't be guided back to its trellis, cut it off. The other parts of the plant will most likely not suffer. In fact, they will probably be relieved of the burden and reward you with new, bushier growth. If annuals have gone to seed, pull them out (unless you plan to save seed from them). Those pyramid-shaped lettuces may look like they have plenty of succulent leaves left to eat, but by now they're bitter and not worth saving. Call a time of death and feed your compost bin.

#### Track Your Canes

This one requires thinking ahead, but if you can tie a ribbon to each berry cane that produces fruit, you will know exactly which ones to cut down to the ground at the end of the season. Blackberries and raspberries grow on second-year canes, canes that have been around for a year, and produce fruit the following season. Once they've done so, it's time to cut those canes down. This trick will enable you to cut away spent canes while giving room to new growth for next year's harvest.

### Tipping Is Okay

It is perfectly acceptable, and even recommended, to cut watermelon and even squash vines if they are out of control. Count two leaf nodes past the fruit and cut or pinch off just beyond that second leaf. The vines can also be moved—after all, they're only attached in one place. Circle the vines around, back onto themselves.

### Pinch Those Suckers

This isn't slang, it's actually the term used to describe new shoots that grow from the axil (where stem and leaflet join) on tomato vines. If left unchecked, they will become branches with fruit all their own. What's wrong with that, you might ask? Suckers are named appropriately because they drain energy away from the fruit. After you have at least four trusses or clusters of fruit, start pinching suckers to help those tomatoes ripen as best they can. If you feel soft hearted as you pull one off, know this: you can root it in soil and grow another entire tomato plant from it if you have room.

## Pruning Cuts

There is one more bit of pruning information that will help you keep your garden in shape. It relates mostly to fruit trees, but can apply to shrubs, hedges, and even some herbs. Knowing which type of pruning cut to use takes the mystery out of pruning. Let's look at the two options:

1. **Heading Cuts—**A heading cut is used to trim a branch back from its tip. By cutting the branch just above a bud or leaf node on an angle, it triggers growth down along the branch. It actually causes a hormonal response. See, the leader tip naturally puts off a hormone called auxin, which prevents the other buds and leaves from becoming leaders themselves. When you cut away the tip of a plant, now the

other buds and leaves can become larger branches. Heading cuts help you fill in bare spots or create bushier hedges.

2. **Thinning Cuts—**This type of cut is used when you want to create more space. Remove a whole twig or branch by cutting it flush with another branch. You don't cut it above a bud, which would stimulate growth. You cut it off at the shoulder. This is the type of cut you would use if you had branches of a fruit tree crossing in the center or touching one another. Choose the branch to keep and cut the other one away.

### GEEKY GARDENING TIP

#### PRUNE LIKE AN ARTIST

When you start pruning a shrub or vine, do what artists do—step back and look at your work occasionally. It will give you perspective on the overall shape, let you see what still needs to be cut away, and perhaps give you added courage to make additional necessary cuts.

Pruning is a huge subject with variances for each plant. Find a good pruning class in your area and keep learning the skill until you feel confident. Some gardeners take classes each year in winter, just in time for winter pruning of fruit trees. Having those regular reminders builds confidence.

Seeds
Seeds
Seeds
Seeds

# CHAPTER 9

# PEST CONTROL

Gardening is all rainbows and butterflies until your first head of lettuce is savagely snatched underground by a gopher, or your beautiful Swiss chard becomes ravaged by aphids overnight. Then it's war. Some gardeners pull out the big guns: pesticides and biological warfare. But it doesn't have to be that way. This chapter gives you the tools to improve your odds against garden pests without reaching for heavy artillery. By using a multipronged approach, you'll spend most of your time enjoying the garden, rather than pulling bottles of pesticides down from the shelf.

## Best Practices for Organic Gardens

As we discussed in Chapter 1, by setting up your ecosystem to include a habitat for good bugs, utilizing regular crop rotation to discourage diseases and pest infestations, and planting a wide variety of crops, you will already be ahead of the pest control game. Daily walks through the garden will also help keep you informed about your garden's predators. These steps are part of Integrated Pest Management (IPM), a system used by organic farms all over the world. IPM also involves knowing something about the life cycle of the pests in your garden, so you can take steps to treat them at the right time. For example, if you know grasshoppers lay their eggs in the soil to overwinter, you can unearth the eggs by lightly digging the soil during winter. You break the life cycle, and drastically reduce your grasshopper problem in the garden. Here are a few other things to ensure a safe growing environment for your plants.

### Clear Diseased Plants

Leaving diseased plant material on the ground can foster another season of disease. Many afflictions like blight or rust live in the soil and come back year after year if plants are not disposed of properly. As mentioned earlier, don't compost any plants that have diseases unless you know your compost bin reaches 160°F. Lower temperatures don't kill powdery mildew or blight infestations, so play it safe and put those in your city's green waste bin. City municipal systems have the facilities to build large piles that get hot.

### Keep Your Tools Clean

Diseases can spread from one branch to another on pruning shears. If you are pruning a diseased plant, dip the blades into a container of bleach or alcohol between cuttings. It may sound extreme, but it's the right thing to do to prevent the spread of many diseases. Clean your tools at the end of each season and disinfect them regularly with alcohol or bleach.

### Use Natural Remedies First

Eco-friendly dish soap mixtures and hand picking of pests can go a long way in the garden. Simple garlic or pepper sprays (puree either with water in a blender and add a few drops of dish soap) will repel a number of pests. A layer of worm castings, with exoskeleton-dissolving chitinase, can solve many problems for you. Diatomaceous earth is another natural remedy that targets soft-bodied insects. It is a white powder made up of fossilized single-cell organisms. It feels like powder to us, but to bugs it's deadly. It pokes holes in bugs, which causes them to desiccate and die. Use a mask when applying and also reapply after rain or irrigation, because it becomes inert when wet. By using these options first, you may never need to resort to over-the-counter horticultural oils or bug sprays. Note that even though USDA- or OMRI-certified organic sprays are safe for use in organic agriculture, some organic products are extremely strong, and just like their chemical counterparts, they don't discriminate between beneficial insects and the ones you intend to exterminate.

In large-scale agriculture, walking the fields and hand picking isn't feasible, so farms use sprays and other protections. In home gardens, however, it only takes a few minutes each day to assess the status of the garden and manage most pest problems without chemicals. One of the best ways to manage pests is by understanding them, so let's look at specific pests and their natural predators.

## Good Bugs Versus Bad Bugs

If you have pests in your garden, there is a good chance those pests have enemies. Beneficial insects are the good bugs of the garden that eat or parasitize bad bugs. It's nature's way of balancing the equation. Here are some of the most helpful insects to include in your ecosystem.

- **Ladybugs** (*Coccinellidae* family)—Those cute beetles with red and black polka-dotted backs are voracious aphid eaters. Ladybug larvae consume about 400 aphids each as they grow into adults, so it's a good idea to attract them to the garden.
- **Lacewings** (*Chrysoperla rufilabris*)—These long, green insects have transparent wings and long antennae. They eat aphids in addition to mites and other soft-bodied insects, as well as scale, which tend to infect citrus trees.
- **Hoverflies** (*Syrphidae* family)—Not to be mistaken for wasps, hoverflies (also called syrphid flies) have yellow and black striped bodies, but are generally smaller

and don't sting. Instead, they focus on eating aphids, thrips, leafhoppers, and mealy bugs. Hoverflies are also good pollinators.

- **Pirate Bugs** (*Orius*)—They don't wear patches over one eye, but they do scavenge the garden for bug booty. They are brown, long, and thin with piercing mouth parts. They feed on spider mites, thrips, aphids, some caterpillars (like corn and tobacco worms), whiteflies, scale, and the potato leafhopper.
- **Tachinid Flies** (*Tachinidae* family)—Appearing similar to a housefly, these bulging-eyed bugs eat aphids and scale. They feed on some caterpillars, grasshoppers, and beetles, and can be parasitic.
- **Gall Midges** (*Aphidoletes aphidimyza*)—These tiny gnat-like creatures lay hundreds of eggs nearby aphids. The larvae inject a poison to paralyze the aphid first, then suck the life out of them, leaving a path of carcasses behind.
- **Parasitic Wasps** (*Aphidius matricariae*)—These are also tiny insects that manage aphids with ease. They can look like miniature flying scorpions when doing their job. They poke holes and lay eggs inside the pest. The aphid becomes a host for young wasps. End of aphid story.
- **Damsel Bugs** (*Nabidae* family)—Commonly found in alfalfa fields, damsel bugs like to snack on caterpillars, leafhoppers, thrips, and aphids. They have similar shape and coloring to pirate bugs.
- **Decollate Snails** (*Rumina decollata*)—We've talked about the benefits of having toads, birds, bats, and bees in the garden, but there is one more creature to include in your arsenal of beneficial insects, though it isn't an insect. It's a gastropod. These snails have a conical-shaped shell, and are cannibals: they eat the eggs and young of regular garden snails. Rather than attract these to your garden, you generally have to import them. Nurseries sell decollate snails in small containers right next to ladybugs and lacewings.

Use the following handy table to match the pest you have with the control solution.

## Pests and Vanquishers

| Bad Bug | What It Looks Like | Who Eats It/How to Get Rid of It |
|---|---|---|
| Ants | You've seen them at your latest picnic | Ants provide a taxi service for aphids in exchange for the "honeydew" aphids excrete. Control ants with borax traps and aphids will decrease. |
| Aphids | Tiny, six-legged, with soft body that is all one color: either green, gray, black, or red | Ladybugs, lacewings, hoverflies, parasitic wasps, pirate bugs, and gall midges |
| Cabbage worm/ moths | White butterflies that lay bright green worms on the undersides of Cole crops | Birds, ground beetles, damsel and pirate bugs, chickens, turkeys. Floating row covers decrease or prevent infestation. |
| Cutworms | Devious earth-colored lumber-jacks that mow down seedlings at soil level | See Geeky Gardening Tip for Pre-venting Cutworms |
| Grasshoppers | Green to brown leafhoppers up to 3" in length | Kestrels, turkeys, rodents, reptiles, and some spiders. Bird netting can be used in some cases. |
| Mealy bugs | White, fuzzy, oval insect coated with powdery wax | Hoverflies, ladybugs, lacewings, parasitic wasps, and mealy bug destroyer. Feed the plant with worm castings to repel them. |
| Scale | Typically light to dark brown armored insect that seals itself to branches and sucks the life out of it | Lacewings, pirate bugs, ladybugs, parasitic wasps, and mites. Horti-cultural oils suffocate scale. Hand removal in small cases. |
| Snails and slugs | Slimy, long bodies with stubby antennae, with or without shells | Birds, decollate snails, chick-ens, turkeys. Submerge shallow dishes of beer to soil level to trap. Replace regularly. |
| Thrips | Thin, pointy-tipped insect with striped body | Lacewings, pirate bugs, predator thrips, parasitic wasps, and mites. |
| Whiteflies | Small, winged, gnat-size flies that occupy undersides of leaves, usually with powdery coating or concentric white circles | Ladybugs, lacewings, pirate bugs, parasitic wasps. Feed affected plants with worm castings to help repel insects. |

# HOMEMADE CLOCHE, A.K.A. MINI-GREENHOUSE

Nothing keeps your direct-seeded babies safer from bugs and cold better than their own mini-greenhouse, or cloche, as it's called by the French (pronounced *cloash* to rhyme with *clothes*). Traditional glass cloches, like the kind used in French intensive gardening, can be prohibitively expensive, and often do nothing to protect plants from cutworms. A simple solution that also happens to be a great recycling project is to make mini-cloches from your used plastic water bottles. These offer more protection than traditional cloches. Here's how:

Remove the cap and ring from each bottle and lay the bottle down horizontally. With a sharp box cutter or mat knife on a solid surface, cut the bottle in two by inserting the knife halfway between the top and bottom, and working your way around the bottle, rotating away from you as you go. When you have finished, you will have two halves. For taller seedlings like green onions or carrots, just cut the bottoms off your bottles and you will have tall cloches in an instant. The top half is ready to use right away, the bottom half needs one more thing—a ventilation hole. Turn the bottom half of the bottle upside (cut side) down. Insert the knife into the top surface and cut out a flap or triangle. Now your plants can get some air and you will be able to water directly through the cloche.

**Mini-greenhouses protecting sprouts and seedlings.**

In your garden, use cloches to cover your seedlings as they emerge from the soil. Push the cloche down into the soil with a twist to create a barrier around the plant both above and below ground. This will keep all sorts of pests at bay: sow bugs (roly-poly bugs), cutworms, snails, slugs, and grasshoppers. When plants have two sets of true leaves, or they outgrow the cover, remove the cloches. When the cloches lose their shape, toss them in the recycling bin. Use eight-ounce bottles for small plants (lettuces, green onions, flowers) and one-liter bottles for wider plants (zucchini and other squash).

## Flowers for Battling Bugs

Now comes the fun part—figuring out how to attract these beneficial insects to the garden. Most flowers attract pollinators, but certain flowers draw insect predators. With a little strategy and careful selection, you will increase your chances of ecological balance and tip the scales in your favor. Here are the most common beneficial insectaries to plant in your garden.

Cosmos, alyssum, and yarrow are all beneficial insectaries.

## Beneficial Insectaries for Pest Control

| What to Plant | What It Attracts | Notes |
|---|---|---|
| *Culinary Herbs* | | |
| Caraway, cilantro, dill, fennel, parsley | Parasitic wasps, ladybugs, lacewings, hoverflies, and tachinid flies | Let them flower. These flowers are umbels, meaning their flowers form the shape of an umbrella. Umbels are generally a good choice for attracting beneficial insects. |
| Catnip, chamomile, chervil, mint | Parasitic wasps, hoverflies | |
| *Vegetables (if left to flower)* | | |
| Carrots and parsnips | Parasitic wasps, ladybugs, lacewings, hoverflies, and tachinid flies | |
| Celery | Same as Carrots and parsnips | Also an umbel when it flowers |
| Cole crops and mustards | Ladybugs and other beneficials | Let them flower; they will attract aphids and subsequently good bugs. |
| *Flowers* | | |
| Alyssum | Ladybugs, lacewings, and parasitic wasps | Low-growing annual that reseeds itself |
| Angelica | Lacewings | |
| Coreopsis | Parasitic wasps, hoverflies, and lacewings | Beautiful yellow flowers |
| Cosmos | Parasitic wasps, hoverflies, and lacewings | Tall, wispy pink or white flowers that reseed yearly |
| Lupines | Gall midges, parasitic wasps, and hoverflies | In the legume family, so they also fix nitrogen in soils |
| Marigolds | Trap crop and repellent for many pests | |
| Morning glory | Ladybugs and hoverflies | In some parts of the United States this is considered an invasive plant |
| Nasturtiums | Trap crop for aphids | |
| Sunflowers | Pirate bugs and parasitic wasps | Flowers produce seeds for birds or human consumption |
| Yarrow | Parasitic wasps, hoverflies, and ladybugs | Perennial flower that is also an umbel |

Choose at least three of the above flower varieties to include in your garden, but the more the merrier. Plant them around the perimeter of raised beds, or in the beds themselves. Tuck them into corners, or plant in pots nearby. Be prepared for your flowers to become a habitat for both good and bad bugs. Better there than in your vegetables.

## Floating Row Covers and Other Barriers

Beneficial insects aren't the only defense you have in the garden. Physical barriers are also part of a healthy garden. Protective coverings like the homemade cloche can mean the difference between survival and decimation for seedlings. Also, farmers use protective coverings to prevent infestations from pests during critical periods of growth, and to stave off frosty weather to extend the growing season.

### Floating Row Cover and Garden Fabric

Two names for the same thing. It is a lightweight, synthetic fabric that allows sunlight and water to pass through, but keeps flying insects from landing on leaves and laying their eggs on the undersides. It also keeps birds from pecking out newly planted seeds. Garden fabric is available in different degrees of protection, from a summer-weight cover to an insulated frost blanket. Use U-pins to hold the fabric in place on top of the soil. Floating row cover can also be installed over hoops to create insulated tunnels along garden rows. Check under the fabric regularly for critters that make it through the barrier.

### Bird Netting

Bird netting is a nylon mesh with 1" openings. It is perfect for covering crops that are regularly visited by rats, squirrels, and of course, birds. Bird netting is nearly invisible and can be draped over strawberry patches, wrapped around fruit trees, and thrown over plants that are going to seed—it keeps critters from invading. Netting is easy to lift for access to your crops or to replant a garden bed. Pin down the corners with U-pins to keep it from flying away in high winds.

Some gardens need above-ground protection from larger invaders, like deer, goats, and neighborhood dogs. Others need underground protection from burrowing creatures like rabbits, gophers, moles, and voles. Here are a few barriers to entry to try.

### Hardware Cloth

It's not really cloth, but metal grid material that can be attached to the bottom of raised beds to prevent burrowing animals from stealing your root veggies. It is best added as the beds are being built. Staple the hardware cloth to the underside (flip the beds over to accomplish this) or use screws with washers to ensure the cloth is securely in place. Gophers can eat through chicken wire, but are less likely to get through hardware cloth. Hardware cloth is worth the extra effort when planning a garden.

### Walled Gardens

It may sound extreme, but for homes adjacent to wilderness, a walled or enclosed garden is the only option if you don't want to share your produce with the wildlife. A 3' wall is only tall enough to keep small critters out, but it's a good starting point. Deer have been known to leap 6' walls to get to delicious produce. Gardeners can build a decorative short wall, but then line the outside of it with deer fencing (thick, 1" mesh) that reaches a height of at least 8'. The fencing will allow sunlight through, and is less noticeable (in the same way bird netting is less noticeable). But that's not the end—dig a 3'-deep trench around the garden and install hardware cloth vertically below ground along the fence. This will prevent burrowing animals from

> **GEEKY GARDENING TIP**
>
> **PREVENTING CUTWORMS**
>
> Cutworms are pests that strike at night when you least expect it. They live in the soil, and surface when it's dark to mow down your seedlings to nubs. Toilet paper or paper towel rolls—cut into 2" lengths—can solve the problem in most cases. Right after planting, shimmy a cardboard collar into place around your seedling and twist it partway into the soil. It blocks cutworms from accessing your plants. If they attack your garden unprotected, dig gently around the damaged area to locate the culprit in the soil; they don't travel far from the scene of the crime.

crossing under the fence. Sure, gophers can sometimes dig 6' down, but most travel only 2–3' below the surface.

### Walk-in Gardens

Some gardens require even more protection than an elaborate walled garden. If you have wild birds that swoop down to claim tomatoes as their own, or wild monkeys who come to visit frequently, you'll need a walk-in garden. It's basically a giant chicken or dog run for your vegetables. Use 2 × 4s to construct a frame, and cover the frame with hardware cloth—top to bottom, overhead and underground. The good news is with a walk-in garden, you can lock the door and you have unlimited trellis space—every part of the enclosure is a growing surface!

## More on Pest-Control Solutions

So you walk out to the garden and find something wrong with your plants, but you don't know exactly what to do about it. You need a place to start. Here is an uber-geeky step-by-step flowchart to help you take action.

Note: This flowchart covers the most common pest infestations but doesn't attempt to diagnose every issue. It also assumes you know what aphids look like. The chart doesn't have an end point, which means you may have to repeat the process for each pest issue several times. Keep in mind that gardening is not an exact science and sometimes your best efforts may work, and other times they won't. Either way, it's best to take a deep breath and try again (eating ice cream helps, too).

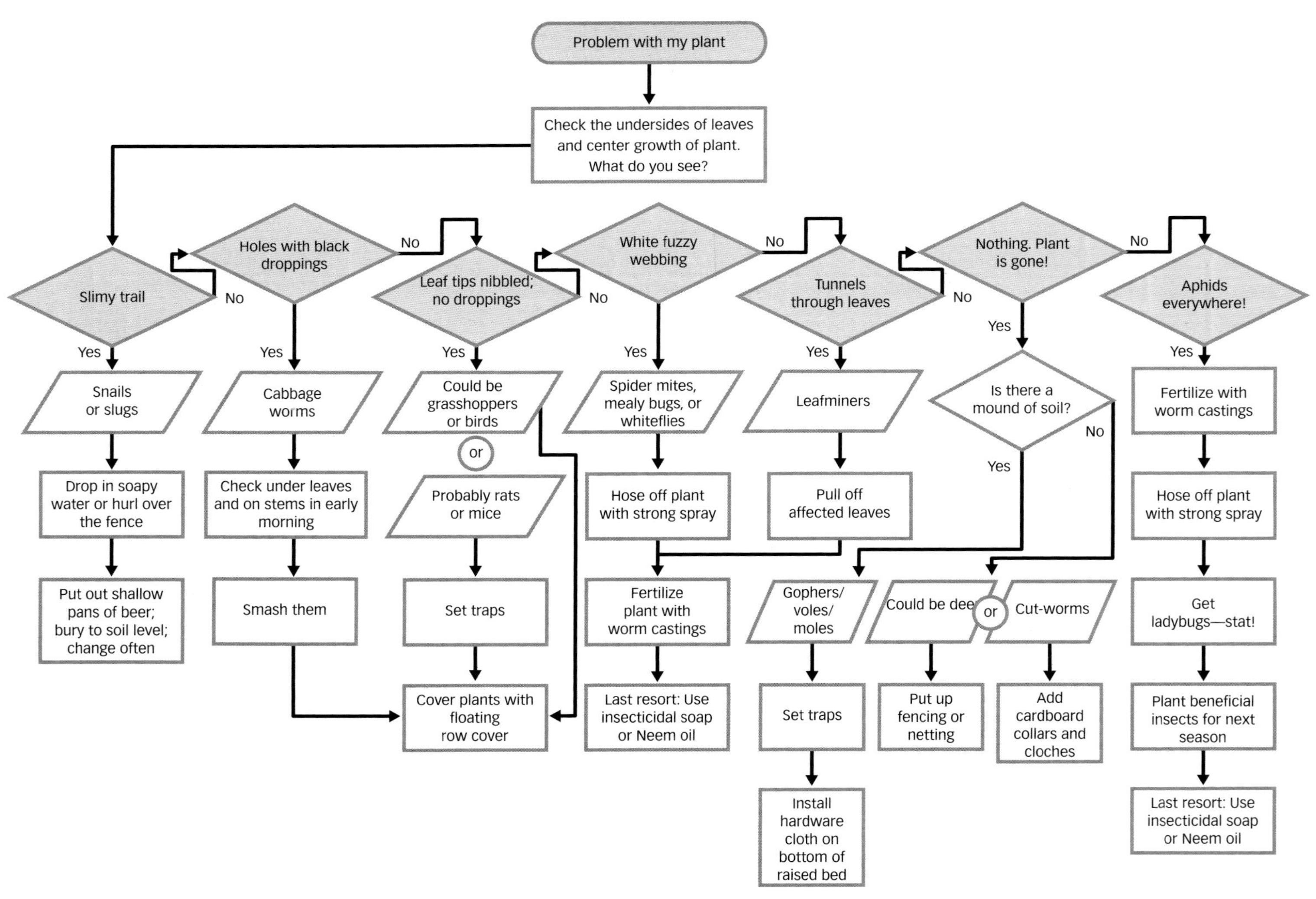
Problem with my plant
Check the undersides of leaves and center growth of plant. What do you see?
Slimy trail
Yes
No
Snails or slugs
Drop in soapy water or hurl over the fence
Put out shallow pans of beer; bury to soil level; change often
Holes with black droppings
Yes
No
Cabbage worms
Check under leaves and on stems in early morning
Smash them
Leaf tips nibbled; no droppings
Yes
No
Could be grasshoppers or birds
or
Probably rats or mice
Set traps
Cover plants with floating row cover
White fuzzy webbing
Yes
No
Spider mites, mealy bugs, or whiteflies
Hose off plant with strong spray
Fertilize plant with worm castings
Last resort: Use insecticidal soap or Neem oil
Tunnels through leaves
Yes
No
Leafminers
Pull off affected leaves
Nothing. Plant is gone!
Yes
No
Is there a mound of soil?
Yes
No
Gophers/ voles/ moles
Set traps
Install hardware cloth on bottom of raised bed
Could be dee
or
Cut-worms
Put up fencing or netting
Add cardboard collars and cloches
Aphids everywhere!
Yes
Fertilize with worm castings
Hose off plant with strong spray
Get ladybugs—stat!
Plant beneficial insects for next season
Last resort: Use insecticidal soap or Neem oil

# UC SANTA CRUZ CENTER FOR AGROECOLOGY AND SUSTAINABLE FOOD SYSTEMS

It's August, and the twenty-five-acre organic farm run by the UC Santa Cruz Center for Agroecology and Sustainable Food Systems (CASFS) is bustling with activity. Apprenticing farmers diligently weed and mulch around fruit trees, while teens participating in a youth empowerment program based at the farm prepare for a tomato-focused farm-to-table dinner. Martha Brown, the center's senior editor, is leading the tour through long beds of cover crops, strawberries, flowers, onions, and more. She explains the different functions of the farm along the way.

In addition to being a historical site where students of Alan Chadwick expanded on the sustainable gardening practices he introduced to the campus in the late 1960s, the farm is also a teaching and research space. The Life Lab Garden Classroom offers the land to young students as a learning tool. Colorful signs explain the science behind composting, a chicken coop sports a diagram of how chickens make eggs, and every flower holds a lesson about pollination or botany. Older students can enroll in a six-month apprentice program to learn Chadwick's methods: double digging, high-density planting, and crop diversity to name a few. A beehive has been on site as long as Martha can remember. A local beekeeper comes to the farm to instruct the apprentices.

Martha points toward a netted area of blueberry bushes, which were planted as part of a CASFS and UC Cooperative Extension blueberry trial. About 180 plants of fifteen different southern and northern highbush varieties are planted in randomized groupings, each row fitted with drip irrigation. When asked how they prepared the soil (blueberries need acidic soil), she explains how they use commercial organic cider vinegar, pumped through the irrigation system, to lower the pH of the soil during twice-weekly irrigation sets throughout the growing season. The bushes were also planted with an acidic wood mulch of redwood and other conifer bark to help keep the pH down. So far, their findings show that Southmoon, Ozarkblue, Jewel, and Sharpblue have done the best for their central California climate.

A little farther downslope, some of the CASFS strawberry fields come into view. These beds are being used to test alternatives to ozone-depleting methyl bromide. Working with the farm staff, the researchers involved in the project are using crop rotation with broccoli, and an application of mustard cake, which is what's left over when mustard is pressed for its oils. Both broccoli and mustard cake contain isothiocynates, which Martha says can help suppress soil diseases, such as verticillium wilt. Studies have shown mustard oils are effective at suppressing nematodes and certain types of harmful soil fungus, so researchers hope to achieve similar results with this approach.

Hundreds of traps are used to keep the population of ground squirrels and gophers at bay. They combat other typical farm and garden problems such as powdery mildew by using drip tape instead of overhead watering. Crop rotation is also a big part of the farm's practices to avoid a buildup of pests and diseases.

A blackboard leaning against a nearby shed lists crops to be harvested. CASFS runs a 100–120 member CSA from early June to early November, coinciding with when the apprentices are there. The twenty-five-acre farm, and the Alan Chadwick Garden, which covers an additional three-acre area of campus, have hundreds of semi-dwarf fruit trees to choose from for the CSA. Persimmons, apples, citrus,

and stone fruits go into the twice-weekly CSA box, along with the typical cool- and hot-weather crops that appear as the season progresses. They also have a CSA cutting garden where members can bring shears and cut their own flowers. Martha says some participants will buy a share and split it with another family. "Our biggest complaint about the CSA is that it's too much food!"

In the off-season they decrease food production and grow cover crops in most of the fields and garden beds. "It's a huge part of our fertility effort," Martha explains. Since they spend part of the year growing nutrient-giving cover crops, they don't try to grow vegetable crops year-round in all the beds. They till the cover crops under with a spader (gentler on the soil than a tiller) or skim them from the beds to use as a compost ingredient, leaving the roots to decompose and provide nitrogen to the soil.

A dibble for planting on 12" centers.

For those who want to run their home garden with the precision timing of a farm or CSA, take a moment to look at the online formula for how much to plant for a successful 100-person CSA (*www.traces.org/green/Course-marketing/4.5_CSA_crop_plan.pdf*). It calculates how many seeds to start, it factors in an allowance for culling substandard plants, or losing plants to gophers and other pests, and it instructs how often to plant in succession for continuous harvest. It also tells you how much land you will need in order to grow it all. Home gardeners can do the math to reduce the formula to garden size.

Inside one of the tool sheds, Martha points to a custom dibble that can be adjusted to automate placing planting holes at specified distances. Back in the beginning, the Home Farmers—the first group of farm students in 1971—used hand tools to double dig the first garden beds, and tilled the first field crops with horsepower . . . from actual horses. They built a mortise-and-tenon barn using no nails. It still stands as a storage shed for farm equipment. The slaughterhouse, a historic structure that was part of the Cowell Ranch's logging and lime-making operation before the university was a twinkle in the public's eye, has since been renamed the laughter house (the "S" in "slaughter" has been ceremoniously crossed out). It shows how the farm's rich history keeps evolving, using time-tested sustainable methods to solve modern-day agricultural problems.

Seeds
Seeds
Seeds

# CHAPTER 10

# NOW PICK IT! (AND THEN WHAT?)

This is the part of gardening most people live for: the part where you get to eat what you've grown. There's nothing like sitting down to a homegrown salad with a colorful array of lettuces, mustard greens, arugula, radishes, and whatever else you like to throw into your salads. It almost doesn't need dressing; it's just that good. A homegrown tomato layered with fresh mozzarella, homegrown basil, olive oil, salt, and pepper is more and more satisfying with each bite. If grocery stores could capture the quality of this experience, we wouldn't need to garden, but there is no substitute for the flavors a home garden can bring to the table.

The joys of growing your own food come with the occasional moment of panic, when you harvest more zucchini, cucumbers, or basil than you know what to do with. This chapter aims to provide solutions for storing, preserving, and yes, using up your harvest. It also offers a few simple recipes that answer the question, "Great, I grew this . . . so, now what do I do with it?"

## Preparing Food for Storage

For a gardener, nothing stings more than spending all season growing your own food only to have it rot in the refrigerator. It happens all the time. That's why it's best to clean or prep veggies right when you bring them in from the garden. Some of these preparations go against what you might typically read about food storage, but they work.

### Fill Up the Sink

Lettuces and other leafy greens will store for weeks if you soak them for twenty minutes in a sink or bowl full of water. Give them room to float around and stir them every once in a while. Soil and grime will sink to the bottom, and plant cells will plump with water. Use a salad spinner to remove most of the water. Place a paper towel or small dishcloth at the bottom of a produce or plastic bag (hate to say it, but plastic bags work better than anything for this task), put your greens inside, and tie the bag closed. Store in the vegetable drawer of the refrigerator until ready to use. After this, salads are as easy as tearing individual leaves into a bowl. You can also go a step further and tear leaves into a large plastic or glass storage container, so all you have to do is put dressing on your greens when you're ready, but they don't last as long this way.

### Keep Certain Fruits and Veggies on the Counter or in the Pantry

Tomatoes, squash, avocados, melons, onions, and potatoes should not be refrigerated. Stone fruits such as nectarines, peaches, and plums should be

stored on the counter until ripe, then placed in the refrigerator drawer. Wash them just before eating.

### Don't Wash Until Ready to Use

Some produce begins to decay quickly if you wash and store it: basil, beans, cucumbers, and peppers. For these guys, brush off any soil and store in the fridge. Then wash them right before you plan to use them.

### Take Off the Tops

Carrots, radishes, and parsnips stay crisp longer if you take the greens off before putting them in the fridge.

### Put It in a Vase

Herbs such as cilantro, parsley, and even basil can be stored like flowers in a vase. If you put a plastic bag over the entire thing and store it on the top shelf in the refrigerator, replacing the water every few days, these herbs will last a long time. Some say asparagus can be stored this way, though others prefer to store it in the fridge unwashed, wrapped in a paper towel in a plastic bag.

### Magic Foil

When you wrap celery in a paper towel, then in aluminum foil, it lasts for a miraculously long time. Just don't forget about it.

If possible, store veggies in clear containers. It is confusing to be greeted by unmarked bags of mystery produce when you open the vegetable drawer. Your food is more likely to be consumed when it's fresh if you can clearly identify it. Many garden geeks label their produce with sticky notes. There's no shame in that.

**GEEKY GARDENING TIP**

**A SALAD SPINNER IS YOUR FRIEND**

If you don't have a salad spinner, get one. It's a gardener's best friend when it comes to preparing produce for storage. The power of centrifugal force spins water off leafy greens, leaving them practically dry for storage. If you don't want to get a salad spinner, you can become one by wrapping your greens in a dishtowel (gather up the corners), walking outside, and whirling your arm around like you're serving a softball game. Just make sure you stand away from anyone who doesn't like to get wet!

## Blanching and Freezing

One of the best ways to preserve your harvest is to blanch and freeze it. It's easy to do and doesn't call for special equipment aside from a stockpot and a bowl of ice water. Let's look at the science behind the process.

Blanching is the act of placing vegetables into boiling water to scald them for a short period of time, usually between three to five minutes. During that time, enzymes—the ones that were hard at work to bring the food to ripeness—are killed. If left to continue, those enzymes would carry on ripening and degrading the color, flavor, and freshness of the food. Boiling water stops the process, essentially stopping time for your veggies.

The process is not complete, however, without the next part. Once boiling is finished, vegetables are plunged into an ice water bath with temperatures below 60°F. The National Center for Home Food Preservation recommends a pound of ice for each pound of vegetables blanched. Place your vegetables in the ice bath for the same amount of time as they were boiled. For example, if you blanch green beans for three minutes, put them into the water bath for three minutes, then remove them.

Once cool, drain the vegetables and thoroughly pat them dry. This step is important because remaining moisture can cause ice crystals during freezing or otherwise damage the food. Here is an at-a-glance chart of processing times for common vegetables. Use the shorter time for small or thin vegetables, and the longer time for thicker vegetables.

### Blanching/Freezing Times

| Vegetable | Time |
|---|---|
| Asparagus | 2–4 minutes |
| Beans | 3 minutes |
| Beets | cook through |
| Brassicas (broccoli, kohlrabi, collards, kale, except cabbage) | 3–5 minutes |
| Cabbage | 1½ minutes |
| Corn (blanch before cutting from cob) | 4 minutes |
| Peas | 1½–3 minutes |
| Potatoes | 3–5 minutes |
| Root crops (carrots, parsnips, turnips, except beets), 1" dice | 2 minutes |
| Squash, Summer | 2–3 minutes |
| Squash, Winter | cook through |
| Sweet Potatoes | cook through |

To freeze your blanched produce, place the vegetables in plastic bags, expel as much air as possible (air is the enemy!), and label them with the date and variety. Store them in the freezer and use them during the winter.

Peppers can be frozen whole, without blanching. Just double bag them to prevent freezer burn. Chop up frozen peppers for cooked dishes and stews.

Some vegetables and fruits freeze better if first frozen in a single layer on a cookie sheet, and then collected into freezer bags for later use. Corn and peas will resist clumping if frozen on a tray first. Soft fruits such as blackberries, blueberries, and raspberries freeze best on a single tray, though they don't need to be blanched first, and apples and figs can be processed the same way. On a side note: frozen grapes are a terrific snack in the hot summer. Just put a cluster of fruit in the freezer and pop individual frozen grapes in your mouth when you need refreshment.

## Drying/Dehydrating

Before the invention of refrigeration, dehydration was one of the most reliable means of preserving food. The process of dehydrating, as the name implies, removes water from fruits, vegetables, and meats. Without water, bacteria and fungi (in the form of yeasts and molds) cannot breed. The result is brittle, perfectly preserved, shelf-stable food that does not require refrigeration. It's a great solution for gardeners with very little freezer space, and in some cases, the end product is better than its frozen counterpart.

There are several ways to dehydrate your harvest, including solar drying and electric dehydrators. From the simplest act of hanging a bundle of herbs upside down to dry in the garage to the more elaborate contraptions like homemade solar food dryers, dehydration is relatively straightforward and inexpensive to do at home. Let's look at the possibilities.

### Air-Drying

For simple herbs such as sage, bay, thyme, oregano, dill, and rosemary, drying is as easy as spreading them out on a screen or paper towel in a room with plenty of air circulation. They may take up to a week to fully dry, but after they become brittle and crumbly you can grind and store them in a glass jar for use in savory dishes. This method of drying should be done out of direct sunlight.

### Electric Dehydration

Home-scale food dehydrators are readily available for the task if you're willing to spend the money. These enclosed units come with five to nine stacking trays that sit compactly on a kitchen counter. You simply load the trays, close the unit, and plug it in. Some dehydrators have timers so you don't forget about your project and end up with unpalatable food pebbles. Good-quality electric dehydrators will cost a couple hundred dollars, but loyal preservation folk will say it's worth the expense.

### Oven Dehydration

Many gardeners and cooks use their oven to dry their harvest. The only caveat is you have to have an oven that can hold temperatures below 200°F. The ideal temperature for drying food is 140°F (though raw food advocates opt for temperatures below 115°F). Some ovens can accomplish this temperature with only the pilot light. If you have an electric oven that begins at 200°F, this may not be an option for you.

### Solar Dehydration

Using the power of the sun to dry food is preferred by many gardeners because the sun's energy is free—there's nothing to plug in. It can be as simple as laying screens of food out on a table or rooftop and covering them with additional screens to keep the bugs away. You can go a step (or two) further by building a solar food dryer to harness the sun's power and incorporate convection, or consistent air current, into the mix. Why convection? Because food dries faster with proper air circulation. Electric dehydrators have a fan to circulate air during the drying process, but the air is simply blasted over the surface of the food. Solar food dryers use convection—heat transfer by the circulation of fluids (in this case, air) to speed the drying process. What would ordinarily take two days to dehydrate in an electric dehydrator can take only one day in a solar unit, depending upon its design.

Regardless of your chosen method of dehydration, it's a good idea to know which fruits and vegetables dehydrate the best. Here's a quick starter list of suitable crops to try:

### Vegetables

Beans
Parsnips
Beets
Peas
Carrots
Peppers, chile and sweet
Corn, sweet and popping
Potatoes
Garlic
Pumpkins
Mushrooms
Tomatoes
Okra
Turnips
Onions (leeks, green, bulb)
Zucchini (sliced very thin)
Parsley

### Fruits

Apples
Pears
Bananas
Stone fruits (apricots, peaches, plums)
Blueberries
Strawberries

When it comes to drying fruit, other factors come into play. Commercial companies use sulfites to preserve color when drying, but home gardeners tend to shy away from preservatives. Instead, some soak fruit slices for five minutes in a mixture of vitamin C powder and water. Drying times vary, depending on the thickness and moisture content of the food. The world of food preservation is immense, and this book doesn't venture to cover every trick of the trade. If you are new to dehydrating, there are plenty of in-depth dehydrating books out there. Check the Bibliography and Resources section for a few suggestions.

# SOLAR FOOD DRYERS

Eben Fodor's book *Solar Food Dryer* is filled with detailed charts on how to capture the sun's energy for preserving food. It has step-by-step instructions for how to build the most efficient solar food dryer possible, and as a bonus, he does it all with recycled materials.

You can too. Here's how:

1. Get the book. Read it cover to cover (it's just over 100 pages). His instructions detail the involved process, but if you choose to accept this mission, the results are completely satisfying.
2. Start scrounging around for wood scraps in the neighborhood, on Craigslist, and nearby construction sites (no stealing, please, but most companies are willing to give you discards). If you have access to Freecycle (a local recycling forum for discarding and acquiring used stuff), look for additional materials there.
3. Go to the hardware store to get any parts you couldn't find recycled (mostly screws and brackets). There is an optional electrical component to the project as well, which allows you to plug in two 200-watt light bulbs at night to keep the process going. It calls for porcelain light sockets (they withstand high temperatures). Most hardware stores in the United States do not carry the size needed for this project, though Fodor reports that Ace Hardware and True Value Hardware stores do. Alternatively, look online for 9880 Leviton Medium Surface Mount Porcelain Light Sockets. You will also need to locate food-grade screen material, which is not made from vinyl like regular window screening. Fodor's website sells it, too (*www.solarfooddryer.com*).
4. Now put on your math cap. Recalculate the dimensions in Fodor's book to account for your recycled materials. His glass window was 27¾" × 30". Let's say yours is long and narrow instead: 48" × 15". You will need to adjust the dimensions for length and width on all related parts, and reduce

your screen size to 2" smaller than your window. Keep in mind with narrow windows, the angle of the glass (to capture the sun's rays) changes.

5. Cut all materials with a table saw. Get help from a carpenter friend or family member if you are clumsy or fear losing a finger. Always wear protective goggles and use a push stick. Note: Don't use plywood for legs or rear braces; use solid wood.
6. Assemble your solar food dryer. Start with the end that holds the legs and interior rails for holding drying trays and a metal absorber plate.

Connect the ends with the cross pieces to create a standing frame. Add the bottom panel to hold the frame square. This may require another set of hands to hold it in place while drilling in screws.

7. Install the electrical backup lighting (if using) to ensure continued drying overnight and when temperatures drop due to clouds or fog. This is highly recommended if you live in an area with coastal marine layer conditions. The lighting elements can keep the unit between 90°–120°F overnight, depending on wattage.
8. Cut, shape, paint, and install the absorber plate. Standard thin sheet metal works great for this project. It cuts easily with tin snips. Making the proper folds in the design can be a little challenging, but if you enlist the help of a friend, it will be much easier to bend sheet metal in a specific place without the use of heavy machinery (hint: use the edge of a piece of wood and four hands).

The book says to paint the sheet metal with high-temperature stove paint. One glance at the back of *that* label may make you shy away from having stove paint anywhere near your food. It off-gasses like mad for a few days, so leave the painted absorber plate out in the sun as long as possible before assembling. As an alternative, you could opt for a nontoxic metal paint. DecoArt nontoxic, no-prep metal paint works like a charm, and is available online and at some craft stores.

9. Finish the assembly—this unit uses natural convection, with screened openings on the bottom and top to facilitate airflow. The top has a vent door to regulate airflow and temperature. The vents are covered with regular screen material to keep insects out. Install the access door and vents.

10. Now for the window. The book uses just the glass part, but if your dimensions include the frame, don't remove it. Attach the window to the dryer and bracket it into place. Use a vice to bend the brackets as needed.

Finished solar food dryer in action, drying leeks.

Add a thermometer for tracking temperatures (requires a small hole in the side of the unit), and your food-safe screens and start dehydrating!

A cheese-making thermometer works perfectly for this task.

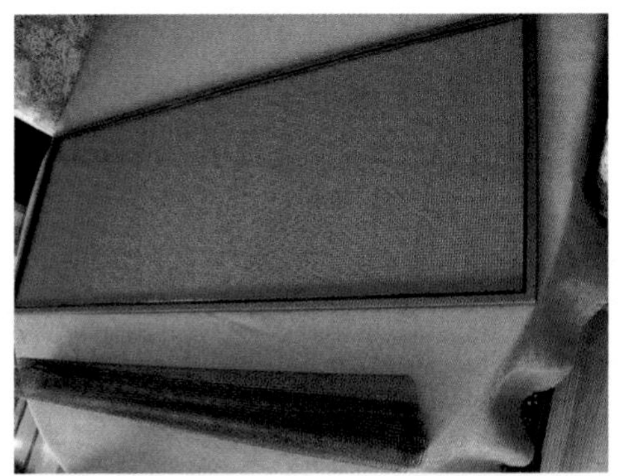

Food-safe screen.

Total cost for this adventure in making the unit featured here was $118.84, including new screening, sheet metal, hardware, electrical wiring and fixtures, and one small hole in the hand (wayward drill). Salvaged materials included the window, screen, wood, some hardware, staples, reflective tape, and elbow grease. Relatively speaking, you can spend $300 or more on a fancy high-powered electric dryer, but you still have to plug it in. Given that it is nearly impossible to find solar food dryers for sale, it makes this machine priceless.

If all of this seems like too much trouble, you can buy the kit from SunWorks at *www.solarfooddryer.com*. Fodor has made it easy to assemble, so you can start preserving your harvest with the power of the sun even faster. Either way, enjoy the process. The satisfaction of building something with your own hands is beyond joyful.

## Canning and Preserving

The practice of "putting up" the harvest has been a long-standing tradition among gardeners for at least a hundred years. Its rise to household popularity, however, came about well after canning originated. The nineteenth-century French government offered a reward to anyone who could come up with a way of preserving war rations for the military. In 1809, Nicholas Appert, a brewer and confectioner, figured it out. He realized sealed food didn't spoil, so he began developing a method to preserve food with heat in glass jars.

We've come a long way since then, but the basics of canning are still the same: the act of boiling closed jars of food kills any existing bacteria and seals the jars at the same time. After that it is shelf-stable. Once it's opened, the food is exposed to new bacteria and can begin to spoil, so it must be stored in the refrigerator.

The terms "canning" and "preserving" are often used interchangeably, but canning usually refers to savory foods or vegetables, while preserving is relegated to fruits (jams, jellies, marmalades, etc.). While this book does not endeavor to relay all of the nuances of canning, use this as a jumping-off point to learn more about the process. Here is some basic information about how to preserve your harvest.

### Start with Clean Jars

Run empty jars through the dishwasher, or wash them in hot water and soap to remove dirt, dust, and hard water deposits. Make sure your jars are free of chips, bubbles, and cracks. Check the rim carefully, because a chip or crack here can prevent proper sealing. Next, place the jars in your canning pot and bring water to a boil. Your canning pot should come with a rack that keeps jars from touching the bottom of the pot. Direct contact can cause the jars to crack, so if you don't have a rack, at least place a folded towel in the bottom of the pot, or improvise a rack by tying together extra bands with string to place on the bottom of your pot. It's like making a trivet out of bands! Don't overcrowd the pot; leave space between jars to prevent them from coming into contact with each other. Boil them for ten minutes (if you live above 1,000' elevation, add a minute for each additional 1,000'). Remove the jars with tongs and set them on dishtowels. Now you're ready to fill them.

### Prep Your Lids

Most canning jars use metal bands that screw on and flat lids that have a rubber gasket. While bands can be reused each year, you cannot reuse lids. The rubber gasket is a onetime-use product. There are also glass or plastic alternatives to these traditional two-part lids that can be reused each year because they come with separate rubber gaskets that can be replaced.

While your jars are boiling, prep your lids. Traditional lids are placed in warm water to soften the gasket a few minutes before applying to the jar. Keep a pan of warm water on the stove with a pair of tongs (or a nifty canning lid magnet) nearby for easy access to your lids once the jars are full and ready to be sealed.

## Leave Some Headspace

Headspace is the amount of room between the surface of the food and the rim of the jar. You need to leave a certain amount of headspace in order to ensure a proper seal. Not leaving enough headspace means your product can swell inside the jar and clog the seal. Too much headspace means you might not get all the air out during processing, which can encourage bacterial growth. Either way, you don't want this. So know your headspace: ¼" for jams and jellies, ½" for tomatoes and fruits (high-acid foods), and 1–1¼" for low-acid foods and meats.

## Then What?

Once you remove your jars from the boiling water, work quickly to fill them to the correct headspace. Use a spatula or chopstick to remove air bubbles from each jar, and wipe the rim with a clean towel to remove any food residue before putting on the lids and bands. This will increase your chances of a good seal. The band should be finger-tight or just tightened. This allows for air to escape as the jars are processed and later as they cool. Avoid over-tightening the jars; they could explode from the pressure created during processing. Place the full jars back in the canning pot and return to a boil. Once a boil is reached, process for the proper time recommended in your recipe.

Remove the jars from the canning pot with the tongs and place them on a dishtowel to cool. When a jar is properly sealed, you will hear a distinct "pop," and the lid will become concave. Any jars that do not seal should be placed in the fridge and consumed first. Once the jars are sealed and cooled, label them with the contents and date. Master preservers recommend removing the bands before storage in order to reveal any hidden improperly sealed lids. Avoid stacking jars for the same reason.

## Water Bath or Pressure Canning?

You might have noticed above the mention of high-acid and low-acid foods. As it happens, the type of food you are preserving determines the method of preservation. Water bath canning is possible with high-acid foods such as tomatoes, fruits, and pickles because they have a pH below 4.6. Low-acid foods such as vegetables, meats, and dairy items require pressure canning to ensure a safe result.

## Use Trusted Recipes

While it's fun to experiment in the garden, canning isn't the time to jump headlong into trial and error. Use proven recipes or take a class to learn how to turn any canning recipe into a safe one. Contact your state's University Cooperative Extension Service to find out if they offer a Master Food Preserver Program. Check out Eat It: Simple Recipes for Homegrown De-lish-es for a trusted tomato canning recipe.

## Eat It: Simple Recipes for Homgrown De-lish-es

The best cookbooks for gardeners are organized by vegetable rather than by salad, entree, and dessert categories. This section offers a few recipes: one recipe for each category of food that makes the most of your abundant harvest of greens, squashes, root vegetables, and more. They are simple and delicious. After all, homegrown vegetables are best when prepared simply, not covered up with scads of sauces, or buried under heavy flavors. These recipes are meant to highlight (or if you prefer, showcase) the flavors of your garden. Anyone can make them, and best of all, each recipe either uses one pan or can be completed in less than thirty minutes.

You'll also find a few recipes for other tasty garden specialties. Impress your fellow garden geeks with fresh pesto, home-canned tomatoes, roasted radishes, and more. Most of the following recipes have come from family and friends, or experimentation based on trusted resources. The goal is to make it easy to use your harvest without much fanfare or work. So let's get started!

### GEEKY GARDENING TIP

#### BPA IN MY CANNING LIDS!?

Bisphenol A (BPA) is used to make many plastics in our world. It also happens to be an estrogen mimicker, which has been proven to wreak havoc on the human body. Sadly, BPA is found in many household products, from thermal paper receipts to the lining of canned foods, to infant toys. While strides have been made to remove BPA from products, it remains as a coating on the inside of some major brand canning lids. Those companies claim their product contains FDA and USDA acceptable levels of BPA. For those who want to take back control, check out Weck glass-lid canning jars (*www.weckcanning.com*), or search the web for "reusable canning lids" for other sources.

# Garlicky Greens with Toasted Sesame Oil

## SERVES 2–3 AS A SIDE DISH

This recipe comes from a fellow garden geek, Carrie Manaugh from Ocean View Farms, Mar Vista, California. Use this with Swiss chard, kale, beet greens, and more mature mustard greens. You can use collard greens and cabbage too, but you'll need to cook them a little longer.

### INGREDIENTS

1 tablespoon extra virgin olive oil

2 cloves garlic, minced or finely chopped

1 bunch (about 12 ounces) Swiss chard (or any kind of kale, beet greens, collards, etc.), stems removed, roughly chopped

1 teaspoon Braggs Aminos or soy sauce

Toasted sesame oil

1. Heat extra virgin olive oil over medium heat in a large sauté pan. Add garlic and stir for 1 minute. Don't let it start to brown.
2. Add chard, drizzle with Braggs or soy sauce, and stir to coat. Cook, stirring often, for about 2 minutes. Chard will reduce in size, but should not be completely wilted. If you want your greens really soft, keep going another 2 minutes.
3. Remove from heat and drizzle with "a whiff" of toasted sesame oil. Stir to incorporate. Serve immediately with your favorite main dish.

# Savory Winter Squash with Sage

**SERVES 2–3 AS A SIDE DISH**

There's no need to mask the savory goodness of winter squash with sugar. These earthy ingredients bring out the delicious flavors and natural sweetness. You'll never go back to sugary squash again.

**INGREDIENTS**

1 winter squash—small pumpkin, kabocha, butternut, acorn, or Delicata

1 shallot

1 tablespoon extra virgin olive oil (use more for larger squash)

1 teaspoon rubbed sage

Salt and pepper to taste

¼ cup shredded Parmigiano-Reggiano cheese*

1. Preheat oven to 400°F.
2. Peel pumpkins, butternut, and other squashes that have fibrous skins. Delicata and some acorn squashes can be eaten with skin on. Slice small squash into ½" moons, larger squash into 1" chunks. Cut shallot into thin slices.
3. Add squash and shallots to 9" × 13" baking dish. Drizzle squash with olive oil and toss with sage, salt, and pepper, using fingers to coat all sides.
4. Bake in the oven for 10 minutes, then stir. Acorn- and Delicata-type squashes, depending on size, may be finished after about 15–25 minutes total cooking time. More dense squashes like pumpkin and butternut will require more time. Cook those another 20–30 minutes, stirring occasionally, until pieces can be pierced easily with a fork. If cooking different types together, put the squash that requires more cooking time in first, and then add the quicker-cooking varieties as you go.
5. Remove from oven and sprinkle with Parmigiano-Reggiano cheese. Serve immediately.

** Vegans can leave off the cheese or use a vegan Parmesan substitute.*

# Tender-crisp Steamed Veggies with a Kick

**SERVES 2–3 AS A SIDE DISH**

Take your pick: this recipe works with broccoli, Romanesco, rapini, cauliflower, green beans, or peas. It's based on a tasty discovery in Dr. Andrew Weil's *8 Weeks to Optimum Health*.

**INGREDIENTS**

1 head broccoli or 8 ounces green beans/peas, rinsed and drained, trimmed as needed

1 clove garlic, thinly sliced

¼ cup water (½ cup for beans and cauliflower)

Extra virgin olive oil

Salt and pepper

Pinch of red pepper flakes

1. Break or cut florets into bite-size pieces. Peel and chop stem into ½" chunks.
2. Place pieces in a pan with a tight-fitting lid large enough to accommodate your chosen vegetable. Add garlic slices. Pour water over the vegetables, then drizzle with about 1 teaspoon olive oil. Sprinkle with salt and pepper and a pinch of red pepper flakes.
3. Put the lid on the pan and bring the water to a boil. Watch and listen closely. When it boils, reduce to a low simmer and cook, covered, no more than 5 minutes (for beans and cauliflower add 5–7 minutes). Turn off the heat and drain remaining liquid. Serve while the gettin's good.

# Romantic Notions of Roasted Vegetables (with Halloumi)

**SERVES 2–3**

You can play around with using carrots, parsnips, turnips, and even potatoes and sweet potatoes here. Throw in eggplant or kohlrabi (cooks like potatoes) and see what happens. Beets have strong flavors, so fair warning—they will influence the overall flavor. Vegetables that take longer to cook are cut into smaller dice, so everything ends up cooking evenly. Eggplant is cut larger so it doesn't get soggy. Halloumi is a Greek cheese that browns and holds its shape when grilled. It's wonderfully salty and elevates this dish to the next level. Throw in some kale and you've got a great meal.

**INGREDIENTS**

1 eggplant, cut into 1½" chunks

2–3 parsnips (5 ounces), cut into ½" dice

1–2 carrots (5 ounces), cut into ¾" chunks

1 kohlrabi, peeled and cut into ½" dice

1 tablespoon fresh parsley (or 1 teaspoon dried)

1 tablespoon fresh oregano (or 1 teaspoon dried)

Extra virgin olive oil

Salt and pepper

3 ounces Halloumi cheese, cut into ½" dice (optional, but a really good one)

5 kale leaves, stems removed

⅛ teaspoon garlic powder

1. Preheat oven to 400°F.
2. Chop vegetables as noted. Rough chunks are perfect for this dish. Place first four ingredients in a 9" × 13" roasting pan. Sprinkle with parsley and oregano, then drizzle with about 2 tablespoons olive oil. Add salt and pepper to taste, then toss ingredients to coat. Bake 15 minutes.
3. While it's roasting, prepare Halloumi cheese, if using. When the timer goes off, add Halloumi to the roasting pan, stir, and return to the oven for another 15 minutes. Chop kale leaves into 1"-wide strips and place in a bowl. Drizzle with 1 teaspoon olive oil and sprinkle with garlic powder. Massage the oil into the kale.
4. In the last 5 minutes of cooking, test vegetables for doneness. They should pierce easily with a fork. Add kale to the roasting pan and finish cooking. Kale should be cooked, with a few crisp edges.

# Sesame Roasted Radishes

**SERVES 2–3 AS A SIDE DISH**

Now we move on to specific dishes that highlight your harvest in a way you might not expect. Radishes have a very distinct flavor when raw, and to some gardeners, that flavor only goes so far. Once you roast them, though, they transform into something completely different. If you were ever on the fence about growing radishes, this recipe will nudge you over. It's a riff on one part of a recipe from Jamie Oliver.

**INGREDIENTS**

1 pound radishes, greens removed

1 tablespoon walnut or peanut oil

1 green onion, chopped

1 tablespoon soy sauce

Toasted sesame oil

Eden Shake (order from *www.edenfoods.com*), furikake, gomashio, or sesame seeds

1. Preheat oven to 375°F.
2. Trim radishes and cut them into quarters. Place them in a casserole dish and toss with walnut oil. Roast until radishes are tender and starting to brown, about 25 minutes.
3. Remove from oven and add green onion and soy sauce. Stir to coat, then return to oven for 5 more minutes. Test for doneness: radishes should pierce easily with a fork.
4. Remove from oven and drizzle lightly with toasted sesame oil. Sprinkle Eden Shake over the top and serve warm.

# Crispy (Addictive) Kale Chips

SERVES 4, OR 1 ADDICT

"What are kale chips?" That's the question that is usually asked when a bowl of oven-crisped kale is put down in front of newbies. They eat one out of curiosity and are surprised to find kale can taste so good. That's all it takes to get hooked.

INGREDIENTS

12 ounces kale, stems removed (curly kale works best, but you can use several varieties for diversity)

1 tablespoon extra virgin olive oil

1 tablespoon apple cider vinegar

⅛ cup nutritional yeast (or more to taste)

Salt to taste

1. Preheat oven to 300°F.
2. Tear kale into 3" pieces (they shrink). In a large bowl, combine kale, olive oil, and apple cider vinegar. Use your hands to massage the leaves until coated evenly. Sprinkle with nutritional yeast and salt and toss to combine.
3. Place leaves in a single layer on two baking sheets. Bake in batches for 15–17 minutes, until crisp, rotating trays halfway through. Curly kale takes longer than Dinosaur/Lacinato kale. Try not to eat them all in one sitting, or at least share with friends.

# David King's Pesto-Madness Pesto

**MAKES ABOUT 4 CUPS**

When you have more basil than you know what to do with, you make pesto. It freezes well and captures the unforgettable flavor of summer. David King, the garden master at the Learning Garden (*www.TheLearningGarden.org*) in Mar Vista, California, developed this pesto recipe over years of trial and delicious error.

**INGREDIENTS**

8 cloves garlic

¾ cup toasted pine nuts

8 cups fresh basil leaves, loosely packed

1⅔ cups Parmesan cheese

2 teaspoons fresh black pepper

1⅓ cups olive oil

1. Add garlic, pine nuts, basil, cheese, and black pepper to a food processor or high-speed blender and pulse to combine. Add olive oil and process just until a puree forms, or process longer for smooth pesto. Scrape down the sides as needed.
2. Use immediately or store in sealed containers with a little extra olive oil on top. The oil will help prevent discoloration. Pesto can be frozen in ice cube trays or single containers. Yummy!

# How to Can Tomatoes

### 1 POUND TOMATOES MAKES APPROXIMATELY 3 PINTS

My mother, Jo Wilhelmi, has always been known for her tomato sauce. It's what brought friends over for dinner. Every batch started with tomatoes that she had canned the summer before. She may not have grown them herself, but she went to a local farm and picked every one of them off the vine. With eyes bigger than common sense allowed, we always ended up with about 100 pounds more than we anticipated buying. Naturally, the only solution was to can them all. This recipe, which comes from her Italian grandmother Antonia, can be used to put up three to 300 jars, and it is best done with friends.

## How to Can Tomatoes, continued

INGREDIENTS

Your fresh tomatoes (at least 1 pound)

EQUIPMENT

Water bath

Colander

Sterilized jars, bands, and new lids

Small saucepan for warming lids

Tongs

Large stockpot

Dishtowels

1. Place washed tomatoes in a large pan; pour boiling water over the tomatoes. Take the tomatoes out of the water within a minute and remove the skins (scoring them beforehand makes it even easier).
2. Cut tomatoes in half or quarters and squeeze out most of the seeds. Place tomatoes in a colander as you peel the rest.
3. Pack tomatoes in jars as tightly as possible with a little juice on top (this occurs naturally). Get the air bubbles out with a plastic knife, thin spatula, or chopstick. Leave ½" headspace. Wipe the rim of each jar.
4. To prepare lids, boil water in a small saucepan.
5. Turn off heat and place lids in the hot water for about 3 minutes. Remove the lid with tongs and place it on the jar, making sure the surface is clean. Screw on the cap, but do not tighten too much.
6. Place a cloth on the bottom of a large stockpot or use a canning rack and put the filled jars in the pot. Fill with water to cover the lids, bring to a boil, and boil, covered, *slowly* for 30 minutes only.
7. Turn off the heat, then take the cover off and let jars sit for about 10 minutes longer in the water. Using tongs, take them out and place them on a dishtowel. Leave them undisturbed for 12 hours. The next morning, jars should be sealed (the center of each lid shouldn't move or click when you press on it). If any jars did not seal, store in the refrigerator and use within the next week.

Seeds
Seeds
Seeds
Seeds

# APPENDIX A

# Browns and Greens for Your Compost Bin

| Browns (Mature Biomass/Carbon) | Greens (Immature Biomass/Nitrogen) |
|---|---|
| Dried garden plants:<br>Cornstalks<br>Grain stalks and chaff<br>Squash vines | Green garden plants:<br>Spent flowers<br>Spent vegetable plants (no seeds)<br>Grass clipping (untreated) |
| Dried tree leaves | Weeds (no seeds) |
| Dried straw/hay | Kitchen scraps (no meat, dairy, fats) |
| Sawdust | Coffee grounds |
| Wood chips | Tea leaves |
| Paper egg cartons | Your hair |
| Cardboard | Your pet's hair |
| Shredded paper | Your chicken's feathers |
| Office paper (no metallic inks) | Animal manures (no dogs or cats—pathogen risk) |
| Junk mail (no glossy pages) | Fresh alfalfa |
| Used tissues | Fresh cover crops—fava beans, clover, vetch, oats, etc. |
| Used paper towels (use unbleached products) | Hedge trimmings |
| Tea bags | |
| Coffee filters (unbleached) | |
| Fabric and lint from natural fibers | |

# APPENDIX B

# Trusted Seed Companies

All seed companies listed here have signed the Safe Seed Pledge. Some offer organic seed, others sell untreated seed. All of these sell heirlooms and open-pollinated seed, with some carrying hybrids as well. Rest assured none of these companies sells GMO seed. In the political landscape of seed companies, some are at risk of going out of business. See *www.Gardenerd.com/links* for updated and additional information on trusted resources.

## Trusted Seed Companies

| Seed Company | Contact Info | Notes |
|---|---|---|
| Abundant Life Seeds | *www.abundantlifeseeds.com* | organic, biodynamic, sustainably grown |
| Baker Creek Heirloom Seeds | *www.rareseeds.com* | the mother of heirloom seed catalogs |
| Botanical Interests | *www.botanicalinterests.com* | family-owned, heirloom and open-pollinated seed; some organic, all untreated |
| Bountiful Gardens | *www.bountifulgardens.org* | retail wing of GROW BIOINTENSIVE; all open-pollinated seeds |
| D. Landreth Seed Company | *www.landrethseeds.com* | oldest seed company in the U.S. (since 1784) |
| Franchi Seeds | *www.growitalian.com* | traditional Italian varieties, heirloom and open-pollinated vegetables, herbs and flowers |
| High Mowing Organic Seeds | *www.highmowingseeds.com* | certified organic since 1996 |
| Hometown Seeds | *www.hometownseeds.com* | small family business specializing in survival seed collections |
| Irish Eyes Garden Seeds | *www.irisheyesgardenseeds.com* | organic seed potatoes, garlic and vegetable seeds |
| John Scheepers Kitchen Garden Seeds | *www.kitchengardenseeds.com* | in business since 1908 |
| Johnny's Selected Seeds | *www.johnnyseeds.com* | geared toward farmers with hybrid, heirloom, and open-pollinated varieties; large selection of garden supplies |
| The Living Seed Company | *www.livingseedcompany.com* | heirloom and open-pollinated seed collections |
| Native Seed Search | *www.nativeseeds.org* | specializing in arid environments and preserving seeds from native cultures in the American Southwest and northwest Mexico |
| The Natural Gardening Company | *www.naturalgardening.com* | oldest certified organic nursery in the U.S.; offers seeds and plants |

## Trusted Seed Companies

| Seed Company | Contact Info | Notes |
|---|---|---|
| Peaceful Valley Farm & Garden Supply | *www.groworganic.com* | seeds and supplies for farmers and home gardeners |
| Pinetree Garden Seeds | *www.superseeds.com* | heirloom, open-pollinated, and hybrid seeds, as well as garden and homesteading supplies |
| Renee's Garden Seeds | *www.reneesgarden.com* | carefully curated seed collections and interesting varieties |
| Seed Savers Exchange | *www.seedsavers.org* | heirloom seeds collected from thousands of members |
| Seeds of Change | *www.seedsofchange.com* | certified organic, heirloom, and open-pollinated seeds; some hybrids |
| Southern Exposure Seed Exchange | *www.southernexposure.com* | strives to preserve seed varieties |
| Territorial Seed Company | *www.territorialseed.com* | some open-pollinated and heirloom varieties; some organic seeds and starts |
| Turtle Tree Biodynamic Seed Initiative | *www.turtletreeseed.org* | biodynamic open-pollinated vegetable and flower seeds |
| Victory Seeds | *www.victoryseeds.com* | will print custom seed packets for your events |
| Wood Prairie Farm | *www.woodprairie.com* | organic seed potatoes and gifts |

## Great Geeky Heirloom/Open-Pollinated Seeds to Try

These are just a few tempting varieties to start you on your way into the world of heirlooms. There are hundreds more than can fit on a page, but these suggestions are fun to grow and interesting to look at while gardening.

| **Fruit/Vegetable/Herb** | **Variety** |
|---|---|
| Basil | Genovese, Big Leaf, Lettuce Leaf, Opal |
| Beans, bush | Dragon Tongue, Roc D'or Yellow Wax, Maxibel, Black Coco (dry) |
| Beans, pole | Christmas Lima, Romano, Cannellini (runner) |
| Beets | Chioggia, Golden, Bull's Blood (for greens too) |
| Broccoli | Thompson Sprouting, Romanesco, Calabrese, Di Cicco |
| Brussels sprouts | Rubine, Seven Hills |
| Cabbage | Vertus Savoy |
| Carrots | Scarlet Nantes, Cosmic Purple, Yellowstone, Tonda di Parigi |
| Cauliflower | All the Year Round, Snow's Overwintering |
| Celery | Utah Tall |
| Chard | Golden, Bright Lights, Fordhook Giant |
| Collards | Vates, Champion |
| Corn | Stowell's Evergreen, Japanese Hulless (popping), Blue Hopi (flour) |
| Cucumbers | Mexican Sour Gherkin, Lemon, Armenian, Early Russian |
| Eggplant | Black Beauty, Listada De Gandia, Rose Bianca |
| Garlic | Kettle River Giant, Spanish Roja, Inchelium Red |
| Kale | True Siberian, Lacinato, Red Russian, Vates Blue |
| Kohlrabi | Early Purple Vienna, Early White |
| Leeks | King Richard, Scotland |
| Lettuce | Rouge d'Hiver, Reine des Glaces, Forellenschluss, Four Seasons, Black Seeded Simpson, Red Oak |
| Melons | Sharlyn, Hale's Best, Rugoso di Cosenza, Golden Honeymoon |
| Mustard greens | Osaka Purple, Mizuna, Tatsoi |
| Onions | White Lisbon (bunching), Rossa di Milano (red) |
| Parsnips | Turga |
| Peas | Oregon Sugar Snow Pea, Sugar Snap Peas |
| Peppers | Jimmy Nardello's (sweet), Corno di Toro (sweet), Ancho (hot), Purple Tiger (hot) |
| Potatoes | Cranberry Red, Rose Finn Apple, Russian Banana, All Blue |
| Pumpkin | Cinderella, Howden, Musquee de Provence, Sugar Baby |
| Radishes | Purple Plum, Watermelon, French Breakfast |

| Fruit/Vegetable/Herb | Variety |
|---|---|
| Spinach | Winter Giant, Viroflay, Bloomsdale |
| Squash, summer | Cocozella Zucchini, Bennings Green Tint Patty Pan, Ronde de Nice Zucchini |
| Squash, winter | Delicata, Watham Butternut, Table Gold Acorn, Lakota |
| Tomatoes | Stupice, Black Cherry, Old German, Great White, Missouri Pink, Green Zebra, Yellow Pear, Garden Peach, Ispolin, Orange Oxheart, Jaune Flamme |
| Turnips | Purple Top |
| Watermelon | Moon and Stars, Crimson Sweet, Sugar Baby |

APPENDIX C

# How to Build an Eight-Plant Tomato Crib

These instructions are similar to those for the four-plant tomato crib. This one is just twice as wide to allow for two rows of tomatoes instead of one. These illustrations also demonstrate how to weave twine for the grow-through trellis.

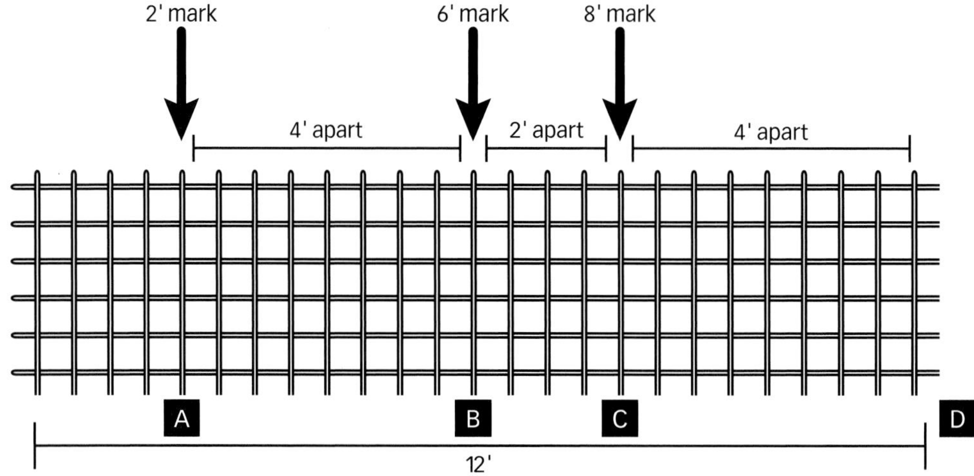


A 12' length of concrete wire mesh is folded at points A–D as noted above. Don't forget to use wire cutters to cut the horizontals off one edge of the mesh to expose vertical spikes that will be your anchors that drive into the ground.

When folding is complete, it looks like this from the top:

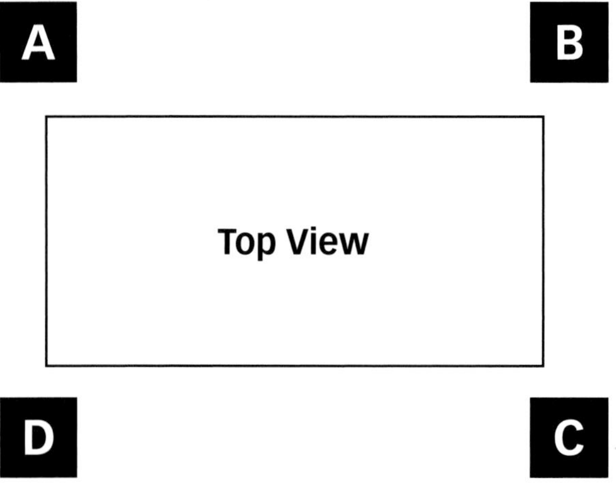


Connect the ends and secure closed with wire. Tomato crib should stand up on its own, with spikes pointing into the soil.

Plant your tomatoes, and situate the crib over them. Next, you're ready to start weaving twine to support your tomatoes.

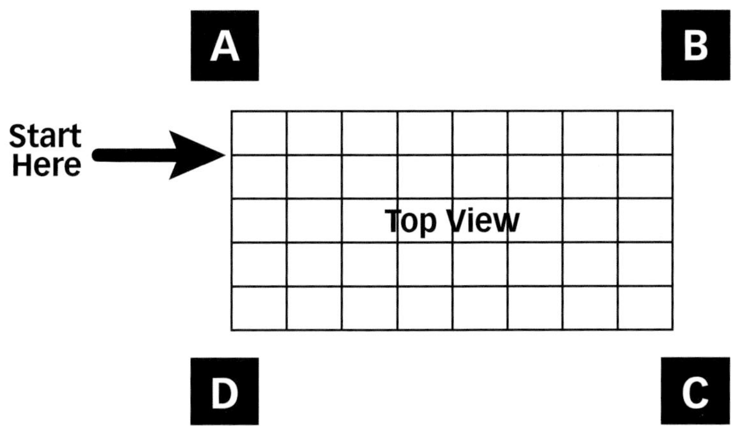


Start at the bottom of one end and weave a lattice across the interior of the crib. String twine along the X axis, then run perpendicular twine across the Y axis to complete the lattice.

As weeks progress and your tomatoes grow, add another layer of lattice above the first one. Repeat each week until the entire crib is filled in.

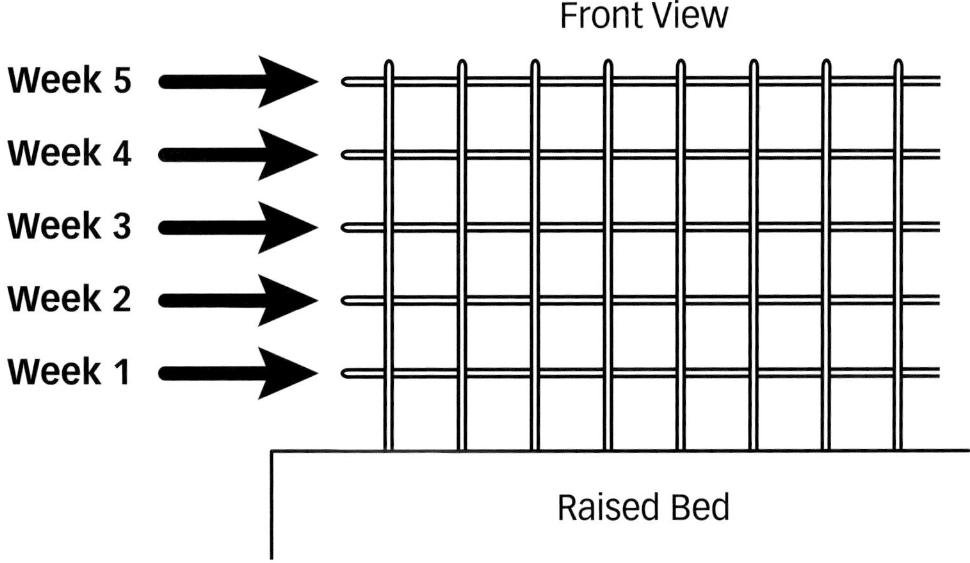


Tomatoes will get support from the very beginning as they grow to fill in the crib. Adding twine each week is easy to do and will help train your tomatoes to grow straight up through the lattice.

# APPENDIX D

# Mounds: Naturally Raised Beds

Simply put, a mounded raised bed is an above-ground pile of organic matter, usually with sloped sides. These beds are at least 6" tall, but can be up to 2' tall, depending on the materials used. Some gardeners stick to soil and compost as ingredients, while others layer different "browns" and "greens," using a method often referred to as no-till, no-dig, lasagna gardening, sheet mulching, or in honor of Ruth Stout, author of *Have a Green Thumb Without an Aching Back*, the Stout System.

It's like building a compost pile straight in your garden, but then you plant in it. Start with newspaper, then add layers of "browns" and "greens" until the pile reaches 2' tall, then top it with compost and water well. Ruth recommended using an 8" layer of "browns," basically any bulky material that could be used as mulch, like hay, straw, sawdust, wood chips, or fall leaves. Her "greens" included garden waste, kitchen scraps, and grass clippings.

You can build a mound directly on your existing soil, but if you have a lawn or grassy (weedy) area, it's best to start with cardboard. Lots of it. One layer is not enough to kill Bermuda or crabgrass/devil's grass; think more like 5–8" thick. That's a lot of cardboard. But let's say, for the sake of argument, that you have weed-free soil selected for your future garden area. You can skip the cardboard and start with a ¼–½" layer of newspaper. What does this do? Once wet and covered with other materials, decomposing newspaper creates the perfect environment, inviting microorganisms to break down the organic matter and till it into the soil for you. It provides carbon, which is one part of the compost equation. It will attract the right kind of fungi to your future garden, the kind that will help make nutrients available to your plants. Water the newspaper very, very well.

Contemporary versions of the Stout System start with newspaper or cardboard, and then add a layer of alfalfa; so this version starts with "greens," meaning nitrogen instead of carbon. Nitrogen-rich materials attract beneficial bacteria to your garden, and they do the work to not only break down organic matter, but they also provide food for other microbes that will arrive a little later. A bale of alfalfa naturally separates into 4" layers, called flakes. While some people prefer to break up the flakes before layering, it's perfectly acceptable to use the compressed flakes on top of the newspaper. One 4" layer is a good starting point. Again, water this layer very well.

For the brown/carbon layers, use twice as much material as your green layer. Variations on the lasagna gardening theme range from adding bone meal or blood meal or peat moss between each layer, to adding compost in the middle or bottom of the stack instead of on top, to using ash or mulch as a finishing layer. It leaves a lot of room for experimentation, doesn't it?

All of these layering techniques require plenty of water as each layer is applied. Straw can take a very long time to become saturated, so be sure to use ample water while building your mounds, or consider soaking it ahead of time. It will become much heavier when wet though, so keep the bale close to its final destination while soaking.

The philosophy behind this particular type of mounded garden bed is that once established, the garden doesn't need water. Granted, its advocate, Ruth Stout, lived in Connecticut where the average rainfall is fifty inches per year. Gardeners in drought-ridden states will need to make adjustments for this. Other benefits of no-till gardening beds include reduced labor, and as the beds decompose, they are feeding the soil beneath them. After a season or two, your garden soil will be much easier to dig, if you decide you want to pick up a shovel.

# Bibliography and Resources

As with the trusted seed company list, these resources are bound to change. Visit *www.Gardenerd.com* for up-to-date recommendations.

## Books and Articles

Allen, Will, Diana Balmori, and Fritz Haeg. *Edible Estates: Attack on the Front Lawn*, Second edition. Pasadena, CA: Metropolis Books, 2010.

Anderson, Arthur B., and Charles B. Wilke. "Solvent Seasoning of Redwood." Oregon State University, 1965.

Bartholomew, Mel. *All New Square Foot Gardening.* Minneapolis, MN: Cool Springs Press, 2006.

Bell, Mary T. *Mary Bell's Complete Dehydrator Cookbook.* New York: William Morrow, 1994.

Bradley, Fern Marshall, editor. *Rodale's Garden Answers*. Emmaus, PA: Rodale Press, 1995.

Bradley, Fern Marshall, Barbara W. Ellis, and Deborah L. Martin. *The Organic Gardener's Handbook of Natural Pest and Disease Control.* Emmaus, PA: Rodale Books, 2010.

Carpenter-Boggs, L., J. P. Reganold, and A. C. Kennedy. "Effects of Biodynamic Preparations on Compost Development." *Biological Agriculture and Horticulture*, vol. 17, (2000): 313–18.

Consumers Union of the United States. "Get the Lead Out of the Garden Hose." *Consumer Reports,* May 2003.

Creasy, Rosalind. *Edible Landscaping.* San Francisco, CA: Sierra Club Books, 2010.

Erv Evans. "Nutrient Content of Natural Materials." North Carolina State University, 2000.

Fodor, Eben. *The Solar Food Dryer: How to Make and Use Your Own Low-Cost, High-Performance, Sun-Powered Food Dehydrator.* Gabriola Island, Canada: New Society Publishers, 2006.

Gardeners and Farmers of Centre Terre Vivante. *Preserving Food without Freezing or Canning*. White River Junction, VT: Chelsea Green Publishing, 2007.

Hamilton, Geoff. *Organic Gardening,* Second edition. New York: DK Publishing, 2011.

Hemenway, Toby. *Gaia's Garden: A Guide to Homescale Permaculture,* Second edition. White River Junction, VT: Chelsea Green Publishing, 2009.

Jeavons, John. *How to Grow More Vegetables*, Eighth edition. New York: Ten Speed Press, 2012.

Kingry, Judy, and Lauren Devine. *Ball Complete Book of Home Preserving.* Toronto, Canada: Robert Rose, 2006.

Kiser, Mark, and Selena Kiser. "A Decade of Bathouse Discovery." *The Bat House Researcher*, vol. 12, no. 1 (2004).

Kourik, Robert. *Drip Irrigation for Every Landscape and All Climates,* Second edition. Occidental, CA: Metamorphic Press, 2009.

_______. *Roots Demystified*. Occidental, CA: Metamorphic Press, 2007.

Lowenfels, Jeff, and Wayne Lewis. *Teaming with Microbes*. Portland, OR: Timber Press, 2011.

Mollison, Bill. *Introduction to Permaculture*. Berkeley, CA: Ten Speed Press, 1997.

Nancarrow, Loren, and Janet Hogan, Taylor. *The Worm Book.* Berkeley, CA: Ten Speed Press, 1998.

Pfeiffer, Ehrenfried. *Pfeiffer's Introduction to Biodynamics*. Edinburgh, Scotland: Floris Books, 2011.

Pleasant, Barbara. "Know When to Plant What: Find Your Average Last Spring Frost Date." *Mother Earth News*, July 30, 2008.

Reynolds, Susan. "Drying Vegetables." University of Florida Cooperative Extension Service Institute of Food and Agricultural Services, 1994.

Rich, Deborah K. "The Case Against Synthetic Fertilizers." SanFranciscoGate.com, January 14, 2006.

Riotte, Louise. *Carrots Love Tomatoes*. North Adams, MA: Storey Publishing, 1998.

Rodale Institute. "Collecting, Keeping Wild Honeybees Boosts Coffee Yield, Adds New Layer of Agroecological Stability." Sustainable Harvest International, March 31, 2010.

Sheikh, Bahman. "White Paper on Gray Water." WateReuse Association, Water Environment Federation, and American Water Works Association, 2010.

Stout, Ruth. "Have a Garden without an Aching Back." *Mother Earth News Magazine*, February/March, 2004.

_______. "How to Grow without Digging." *Organic Gardening Magazine*, vol. 58.1, p. 49.

Waskom, R. M., T. Bauder, J. G. Davis, and A. A. Andales. "Diagnosing Saline and Sodic Soil Problems." *Fact Sheet Number 0.521*, Colorado State University Extension, July 2003.

## Websites and Organizations

American Community Garden Association
*www.communitygarden.org*

Backwards Beekeeping
*www.backwardsbeekeepers.com*

The Bug Guide
*www.bugguide.net*

Institute for Responsible Technology
*www.responsibletechnology.org*

Slow Food
*www.slowfood.com*

Yardsharing
*www.hyperlocavore.ning.com*

# Glossary

**Annual/Perennial**—A plant that completes its life cycle in one season or year is an annual. It dies when it's finished growing and is replaced the following year. Perennials are longer-lasting plants that live more than a year. A tree is a perennial. Sweet basil is an annual. So when an annual dies at the end of the season, it's not your fault; it's what nature intended.

**Axil**—The upper angle between the leaf and stem of a plant.

**Berm Beds**—A berm is a raised planting area, which stands out from the rest of the garden by reason of being raised. Berm beds, then, are beds planted on berms.

**Biodynamics**—The term used for a holistic approach to agriculture that emphasizes natural methods of growing and fertilizing and stays away from artificial pesticides and soil additives. Biodynamic gardening tries to integrate all aspects of the ecosystem in the garden, including plants, animals, and irrigation. It was first proposed by Rudolf Steiner in the 1920s.

**Biomass**—Biological material from living (or recently living) organisms. For the purposes of this book, biomass includes mature (dried/dead carbon-rich) materials such as fallen leaves, and immature (living nitrogen-rich) materials such as green garden waste and kitchen scraps.

**Bolt to Seed**—When a plant is stressed by hot weather or not enough water, or is at the end of its life cycle, it begins to elongate, sending up a flower stalk from the center of the plant. A seed head forms at the top—a last gasp to produce offspring before dying. Most plants lose flavor or become tough and bitter when this occurs. Bolting to seed indicates that it's time to pull out the plant and compost it.

**Coir**—A fiber taken from coconut husks. It's used in many products, but in gardening it can be used as a substitute for peat moss.

**Compost Tea**—A water solution that contains nutrients from compost, as well as a multitude of beneficial soil microbes. Essentially, it concentrates the biological benefits of compost. You can find many recipes for brewing compost tea online.

**Direct Seeding**—When you sow seeds in the ground exactly where you want them to mature, this is called direct seeding. Plants that have trouble germinating or are sensitive to cold weather prefer to be started indoors in seed trays. Many crops can be direct seeded: lettuces, greens, root crops, and non-woody herbs are the easiest.

**Earthbags**—Polypropylene bags that are filled with soil and used as building material. Some architects refer to this technique as superadobe because they fill the bags with adobe, or heavy clay soil. The technique has become more popular during the past decade.

**Emitters**—Simply put, emitters are the places in drip tubing where water comes out. There are different types of emitters: in-line emitters, which are built into the tubing, and on-line emitters, which are attached to the outside of tubing. Drip tubing is available with emitters spaced 6, 12, 18, or 24 inches apart.

**Inoculant**—Inoculant is a black powder that is used to coat bean and pea seeds before planting. The inoculant introduces rhizobia bacteria into the soil, which allows the legume roots to begin forming nodules for fixing nitrogen. Once soils are populated with these bacteria, you don't need to use inoculants again. If you are planting in a new area each year, though, use inoculants as you sow bean and pea seeds.

**Loam**—Soil that's made up of more or less equal proportions of sand, silt, and clay is called loam. It's the type of soil that is great for gardening and is the goal that every gardener strives for when working amendments into the soil.

**Monoculture**—Some farmers produce a single kind of crop in a given area for many years. Although big agricultural firms use this technique, it's anathema to small farmers and gardeners who are concerned with biodiversity and the health of the soil.

**Ollas**—Ollas are unglazed jugs with long necks that are buried in the ground, leaving only the jug's open mouth exposed. Gardeners fill the jugs with water, which seeps through porous walls into the soil right where the roots need it.

**Permaculture**—A set of principles or design tools created by Bill Mollison and David Holmgren used to develop ecological systems. These principles are applied to architecture, agriculture, and self-reliance, to work in concert with nature and restore balance to damaged landscapes.

**Potting Soil**—As mentioned earlier, there's no actual soil in potting soil. Instead, it contains decomposed organic matter and perlite, which helps drainage of the "soil." Potting soil also often contains peat moss or coir.

**Three Sisters Garden**—This is a Native American tradition of interplanting beans, corn, and winter squash together. The Iroquois understood that these three plants were beneficial companions. Beans use the corn as a trellis, corn benefits from nitrogen-fixing beans, and squash plants provide a living mulch with their broad leaves. Corn is planted first, then beans are planted next to each cornstalk, then squash is planted around the perimeter of the planted area to provide shade for the root systems.

**Tilth**—A gardening term used to describe soil that has the right structure and nutrients to grow stuff, tilth is related to the word "till," as in "till the soil."

**Tree Collard**—This perennial vegetable is part of the brassica family. It is a bit sweeter than related veggies such as kale. Tree collard is also unusual in that it grows to be as tall as eleven feet. It is an integral part of a Grow Biointensive or Permaculture garden as a perennial food source.

**Unconstructed Bed**—Another term for these beds is open mound beds. They don't have sides and can be built up to be six inches or more above ground level.

**Volunteer(ing)**—A plant that grows all by itself, from seeds unknown, is a volunteer. If vegetables are left to go to seed in the garden, the likelihood of volunteering is much higher. Some gardeners let cilantro, arugula, and dill go to seed each year in hopes of having an abundant volunteer crop next season. Many times, volunteers grow to be stronger and more prolific than anything planted deliberately. I like to call them "nature's slap in the face."

# Index

Note: Page numbers in *italics* indicate plant profiles. Page numbers in **bold** indicate recipes.

## About the Author

Christy Wilhelmi empowers people to grow their own food, to be more self-reliant, and to reduce pollution and waste, one garden at a time. Christy is founder of Gardenerd (*www.Gardenerd.com*), the ultimate resource for garden nerds, where she publishes newsletters, her popular blog, and podcasts. She specializes in small space, organic vegetable garden design and consulting. She teaches organic gardening classes throughout Los Angeles, at Santa Monica College, and has co-taught an organic gardening workshop at the Esalen Institute in Big Sur, California. Christy has been a board member of Ocean View Farms Organic Community Garden in Mar Vista, California, since 1999 and gardens almost entirely with heirloom vegetables. Between 70 and 80 percent of her family's produce comes from her garden of less than 200 square feet. Her writing has appeared in *Edible Los Angeles* and *Edible Westside* magazines, *The Good Food Blog*, and LowImpactLiving.com, and she writes the *Mar Vista Farmers' Market Wrap-Up* for Patch.com.